My French Kitchen

My French Kitchen

A BOOK OF 120 TREASURED RECIPES

Joanne Harris

& Fran Warde

WM

WILLIAM MORROW

An Imprint of HarperCollins*Publishers*

Other books by Joanne Harris
Gentlemen and Players
Jigs & Reels
Holy Fools
Chocolat
Coastliners
Five Quarters of the Orange
Blackberry Wine
Sleep, Pale Sister

Other books by Fran Warde
Food for Friends
Eat Drink Live
Thirty-Minute Italian

This book was originally published as *The French Kitchen: A Cookbook* in England in 2002 by Transworld Publishers, a division of The Random House Group Ltd.

A hardcover edition was published in 2003 by William Morrow, an imprint of HarperCollins Publishers.

HarperCollins books may be purchased for educational, business, or sales promotional use. For information please write: Special Markets Department, HarperCollins Publishers, 10 East 53rd Street, New York, NY 10022.

First William Morrow paperback edition published 2006.

APR 7 2006

The Library of Congress has cataloged the hardcover edition as follows:

Harris, Joanne, 1964–
    My French kitchen / Joanne Harris and Fran Warde.
      p. cm.
    ISBN 0-06-056352-4 (hc. : alk. paper)
      1. Cookery, French. I. Warde, Fran. II. Title.

TX719.H267 2003
641.5944—dc21   2003045871

ISBN-13: 978-0-06-082094-7 (pbk.)
ISBN-10: 0-06-082094-2

06 07 08 09 10 WBC/IM 10 9 8 7 6 5 4 3 2 1

Contents

Introduction

Many of my earliest memories are about food. I remember making pancakes with Mémée, my great-grandmother, in her house in Vitré when I was three years old. I remember making jam with my grandfather in Barnsley, and picking blackberries to make wine. I remember my Yorkshire grandmother's rhubarb and apple pie, and my French grandmother's green fig jam. I remember long childhood holidays on the island of Noirmoutier, going around the markets in the early morning or cooking sardines on a charcoal brazier on the sand, and I remember *poule au pot* in Gascony with my grandfather's old friends the Douazans. So many memories are associated with the tastes and smells of cooking; so many places, so many people can be brought to life using nothing more than a handful of herbs or an old recipe.

It's astonishing how much of our past and our culture are secretly defined by food. Our earliest sensations are to do with tastes and smells; as infants we experience food as comfort, food as an expression of love. Later we make our own associations, but for me, the kitchen has always been the heart of my family, a place where the family assembles, not just to eat but also to be together, to talk, to put the world to rights, to teach, to remember the past, to watch and learn.

My kitchen is essentially French in character. There's a strong tradition of cooking on my French side, handed down from my great-grandmother. My mother, too, is a terrific cook, and when she arrived in Yorkshire—speaking virtually no English and feeling, inevitably, a little homesick—she used the familiar recipes to remember the people at home, to remind herself of who she was, and to keep in touch with her cultural identity.

As far as I know, my father had no difficulty in adjusting to this radical change of diet. However, married as I am to a vegetarian (and with a militant 8-year-old veggie daughter), I have discovered that sometimes cultures clash. Not that I have anything against vegetarianism. I enjoy vegetarian food, and when I am at home I rarely cook anything else. But food is as much about heritage as it is about taste; and the French half of me refuses to let go of so large a section of my past. As a result, this book is a kind of family album, in which every recipe paints a picture, as well as, I hope, an introduction to some of the regional flavors of France.

Cooking is a social activity. My mother's kitchen—and my grandmother's, and my great-grandmother's—was open to all comers. My grandmother sang constantly (and very tunelessly) as she peeled potatoes. My mother told stories. There were forbidden areas (my great-aunt Marinette's pancake pan, for instance, was formally out of bounds), but for the most part the kitchen was a learning zone for children, a place where philosophies were expounded, histories examined, and scandals unearthed. Inevitably, much of my childhood seems to have taken place in and around kitchens. The recipes in this book are mostly

French because my main influences come from there, mostly traditional because they have been handed down over many years, and mostly very simple to make. When the ingredients are really good, simple food works; there is no need for complicated sauces or fiddly garnishes. Traditional food demands respect and attention to quality, and this, I think, is the principal ingredient of the French kitchen.

Regardless of other differences, on this subject my English and my French sides are in complete agreement. Food—and its preparation—should be a pleasure. Faced with such a bewildering selection of "conveniently" processed foods and ready meals in the supermarkets, it is sometimes hard to remember this. There is nothing convenient about bad food. When in a hurry, it still takes less time to make a fabulous salad or sandwich or pasta dish than it does to defrost an overpriced tray of mush. So take a little time in selecting your ingredients; go out of your way to find a really good organic butcher or cheesemonger or baker. Visit markets instead of supermarkets. Rediscover the joy of eating locally grown produce in season, instead of food flown in from the other side of the world. Try growing your own herbs (lack of space is no excuse—even a windowsill will do). If you are lucky enough to have a garden, then you may already have discovered the difference between home-grown and far-flown; if not, try a couple of life-enhancing rows of carrots or spinach or raspberries or a pot of some impossible-to-find variety of tomato. Brought up alongside my grandfather's allotment in Yorkshire, I developed this addiction to home-grown food early in life, and I am still amazed at the number of people who think that tomatoes are round and red and tasteless (as opposed to green and sweet and stripy, or long and yellow and tangy, or orange and lumpy and fantastic), or that most unidentified things taste like chicken, or that strawberries have a uniform shape. Food is a sensual, whole-body experience: look at what you are cooking, smell the ingredients, mix them with your fingers. Enjoy their sounds and textures. Bear in mind that cooking is about as close to magic as modern society allows: to take a set of basic ingredients and to transform them into something wonderful, something from another part of the world. Most of all, have fun. Bring your friends into the kitchen; ask your family to help. Let your children watch. Enjoy it together.

Salads

Many people, on seeing the word "salad" in a cookbook, will tend to shudder and pass quickly on to the section marked "chocolate." This is because for many years salads have had a rather bad press, and have been associated mainly with dieting and the depression that often follows. However, French salads take us far beyond these stereotypical wet-lettuce-and-celery-stick meals and into an area of vast and delicious diversity. For a start, salads do not have to contain lettuce. They do not even have to contain vegetables, although they do provide a wonderful means of making the most of the seasonal fruits and vegetables that are one of the principal beauties of a French market. Salads may be served warm or cold and contain raw or cooked ingredients, but will most often be served with some form of dressing, usually containing lemon juice, vinegar, oil, and spices.

I remember being taught to prepare a vinaigrette when I was about four years old—it's that easy. To three tablespoons of oil, add one of vinegar, plus another of mustard. Add salt and pepper to taste, then mix well with a fork. You can use other ingredients to vary the taste: balsamic or grainy mustard, herbs, chiles, garlic, or different types of oil and vinegar. The results can be dramatically different; walnut or pistachio oil, for instance, gives an entirely different flavor to a goat cheese salad, or try adding a splash of raspberry vinegar to a summer salad for a fresh, sweeter taste.

The beauty of salads is that the variations are almost endless. Crisp leaves and herbs, sliced fruit, grated carrots, seeds, olives, cheeses, warm potatoes with olive oil, capers and garlic dressing, marinated duck or salted fish—all these work very well, and you can vary your combinations according to the season or to suit your personal taste. They are extremely easy to prepare, and for the most part, very quick, and it is for this reason that I make so many salads, both in winter and in summer. My favorites are among the simplest: raw porcini mushrooms, thinly sliced and served with lemon, a little salt, and a drizzle of olive oil; fat ripe tomatoes, warmed on a sunny windowsill and served sliced with a vinaigrette and chopped parsley; grated carrots with parsley, oil, and lemon. These are the most basic of recipes, but they can be truly spectacular if the ingredients are good enough, and serve to remind us how wonderful some foods can be with only a minimum of fuss and preparation.

Salads are easy, quick, and endlessly variable. Despite being among the most basic of recipes, the results can be wonderful: as good on the eye as on the tongue. The better the ingredients, the better the results, so shop carefully, or grow your own.

I adore this dish. It's so simple, but the flavors and smells of it take me right back to holidays in France by the sea, and to the little goat farm on Noirmoutier where my mother always bought our cheeses.

Warm Goat Cheese Salad Serves 6

There are different types of goat cheese—such as the delightfully named *crottins de chèvre*—but for this recipe it's better to use the *bûche,* or log-shaped, cheeses. There is a wonderfully earthy taste to good goat cheese, which when mixed with really fresh salad leaves, crunchy walnuts, and good, spicy olives evokes the spirit of summer.

10 ounces log-shaped goat cheese—the best you can find
6 baguette slices
8 cups mixed salad greens (mesclun)
4 ounces black niçoise olives, pitted
½ cup (2 ounces) walnuts

For the dressing
2 tablespoons cider vinegar
1 teaspoon grainy mustard, such as Meux
1 teaspoon Dijon mustard
Sea salt, to taste
Freshly ground black pepper, to taste
⅓ cup plus 1 tablespoon extra-virgin olive oil

Heat the broiler.

Cut the goat cheese into six equal rounds and put one on top of each slice of baguette. Put them on the broiler rack but do not broil yet.

Put the vinegar, mustards, and salt and pepper in a covered jar and shake vigorously until smooth. Add the olive oil and shake again to blend. Pour the dressing into a mixing bowl, add the greens, olives, and walnuts, and toss well. Put the baguettes with the cheese under the broiler and cook for 2 minutes, until the cheese is coloring and bubbling. Serve at once on a bed of greens.

Wild Mushroom Salad Serves 6

If you can't find imported fresh porcini (sometimes known by their French name, *cèpes*), use other wild varieties, such as horn of plenty, chanterelle, or morel, or good cultivated mushrooms.

6 fresh medium porcini mushrooms
Olive oil for sautéing
7 ounces slab bacon, diced
½ cup dry white wine
1 tablespoon balsamic vinegar
3 garlic cloves, chopped
Sprinkling of paprika
Bunch of flat-leaf parsley, chopped
Sea salt, to taste
Freshly ground black pepper, to taste
8 cups mixed salad greens (mesclun)
2 tablespoons extra-virgin olive oil
6 thin baguette slices, toasted

Break the stalks of the mushrooms away from the caps, trim the ends, and brush away any dirt. Don't wash the mushrooms.

Heat a little olive oil in a large skillet, add the mushroom stalks and caps, and cook for 5 minutes, until golden brown. Remove the mushrooms from the pan with a slotted spoon, add the bacon, and cook until golden. Then return the mushrooms along with the wine, vinegar, garlic, paprika, parsley, salt, and pepper, and simmer for 8 minutes, adding a little water if the liquid evaporates and the pan threatens to become dry.

Meanwhile, toss the salad greens in the extra-virgin olive oil. Put the toasts on a plate, cover with the salad, and serve the mushrooms on top, with any juice from the pan drizzled over.

A little bacon fried in a pan not only renders fat but also adds flavor. You need good slab bacon. Don't bother with pre-sliced—it's too thin. Buy thick-cut from your butcher, or get a 1-pound slab, keep it refrigerated, and cut off ⅛-inch-thick slices when needed. Remove the skin and dice the flesh into perfect chunks of bacon.

Green Bean Salad: a perfect light meal on its own, as well as the ideal accompaniment to more elaborate dishes. The thin beans have a wonderful, slightly floury texture that is ideal for use in salads: they absorb flavors and melt in the mouth. Don't add salt during cooking, though—it toughens the skins.

799 PF 16

White Bean and Tomato Salad Serves 6

Haricots Blancs en Salade goes really well with grilled fillets of fish, turning a simple dish into something special.

1 pound small red- or white-skinned new potatoes
1 pound ripe tomatoes
4 (15- to 19-ounce) cans white kidney (cannellini) beans, drained and rinsed (see Note)
4 scallions, white and green parts, finely sliced
Bunch of flat-leaf parsley, roughly chopped
1 hot red chile, finely diced (include the seeds if you like it hot)
4 tablespoons extra-virgin olive oil
Zest and juice of 1 lemon
Sea salt, to taste
Freshly ground black pepper, to taste

Cook the potatoes in their skins in a saucepan of lightly salted simmering water for 20 minutes. Drain and allow to cool, then cut into wedges. Dip the tomatoes in a saucepan of boiling water for 20 seconds, peel, cut into wedges, and remove the seeds. Mix the potatoes, tomatoes, and drained beans.

Combine the scallions, parsley, and chile, then mix with the olive oil, lemon zest and juice, salt, and pepper. Pour over the tomatoes, beans, and potatoes; mix well and serve immediately.

Note: If you wish, substitute 4 ounces dried white kidney (cannellini) beans for the canned beans. Soak the beans overnight in a saucepan of cold water. The next day, drain them, rinse well, and return them to the pan. Cover with water, bring to a boil, and simmer for 1 hour. Skim off any froth that rises to the top during cooking. Drain and cool.

Green Bean Salad with Pine Nuts and Feta Serves 6

This is a cheerful, easy-to-make salad—*Haricots en Fête*—which my vegetarian husband can eat as a main course without feeling too left out.

1 pound green beans, trimmed
⅓ cup pine nuts
7 ounces feta cheese, crumbled
4 ounces black Mediterranean olives, pitted
Bunch of flat-leaf parsley, finely chopped
5 tablespoons extra-virgin olive oil
Juice of 1 lemon
Sea salt, to taste
Freshly ground black pepper, to taste

Plunge the beans into a pan of lightly salted boiling water, cook for 2 minutes, then drain and refresh in cold water until the beans are cold. Drain and dry them, and place in a large salad bowl.

Cook the pine nuts in a nonstick skillet over medium heat until golden all over. Be warned: nothing seems to happen for a while, then all of a sudden the pine nuts will color very quickly. Add the pine nuts to the beans along with the feta, olives, and parsley. Add the olive oil, lemon juice, salt, and pepper; mix well and serve at once.

Warm Tuna and Potato Salad   Serves 6

This is a fabulous salad for winter or summer, full of different textures and rich flavors. It's excellent as a main course—try serving it in a large dish in the center of the table, with plenty of crusty bread.

For the dressing
2 shallots, finely diced
3 tablespoons white wine vinegar
2 tablespoons grainy mustard, such as Meaux
Sea salt, to taste
Freshly ground black pepper, to taste
⅓ cup plus 2 tablespoons extra-virgin olive oil

1 pound small red- or white-skinned potatoes
6 ounces *haricots verts* or thin green beans, trimmed
Olive oil for the pan
8 ounces cherry tomatoes
6 ounces tuna in olive oil, drained
4 salt-packed anchovies, filleted and cut lengthwise
    into thin strips
1 large bunch of basil

For the dressing, put the shallots, vinegar, mustard, salt, and pepper into a jar with a tight-fitting lid and shake until well blended. Then add the olive oil and shake vigorously again. Shake well before using.

Gently cook the potatoes in their skins in a saucepan of lightly salted simmering water for 20 minutes.

Drain the potatoes, cut them in half, and place them in a salad bowl. Pour the dressing over and toss to coat the warm potatoes.

Plunge the green beans into lightly salted boiling water and cook for 2 minutes. Drain well and add warm to the potatoes.

Meanwhile, heat the oven to 400°F. Lightly brush a baking sheet with olive oil. Toss the cherry tomatoes in the oil to coat them and roast for 10 minutes. Add the hot tomatoes to the potatoes and green beans.

Flake and add the tuna along with the anchovy strips and gently mix. Tear up the basil, scatter it over the salad, and serve at once.

A small but key part of this dish is the anchovy. Tiny fish that are abundant in the Mediterranean, they are rarely found fresh but are instead sold preserved in salt or olive oil, either whole or in fillets. Watch for salt-preserved anchovies. They are less easy to find, but they are the best. Soak the whole anchovies in cold water for 10 minutes, then drain and fillet. Once the jar or can is opened, store anchovies in the refrigerator.

I like to keep an open mind when shopping for food.
Markets are the best places in which to find beautiful,
fresh vegetables and salad ingredients, so be creative
and let yourself be seduced by what is on display.

Frisée with *Lardons*   Serves 6

Frisée is one of the joys of a French summer market. As large and curly as a bouquet of chrysanthemums, it has a lovely texture and more taste than ordinary chicory. The combination of fresh lettuce, fried lardons (bacon cubes), and warm, creamy poached-egg topping is cheery and irresistible.

1 large head frisée
2 shallots, diced
Olive oil for frying
½ baguette, cut into cubes
1 pound slab bacon, cubed (see page 19)
6 large eggs

For the dressing
2 tablespoons red wine vinegar
2 tablespoons Dijon mustard
Sea salt, to taste
Freshly ground black pepper, to taste
2 tablespoons extra-virgin olive oil

Break up the frisée, wash and spin it dry, and place in a large bowl with the shallots.

Heat a little olive oil in a skillet and fry the bread in batches until golden on all sides, then remove from the pan and place on paper towels. Wipe out the pan, add a little more olive oil, and fry the bacon for 8 minutes, or until golden.

To poach the eggs to perfection, bring a pan of water to a gentle simmer. Carefully break in the eggs, return the water to a simmer, then immediately remove the pan from the heat. Cover it with a lid and let it sit for 5 minutes.

Put the vinegar and mustard along with the salt and pepper into a jar with a tight-fitting lid and shake vigorously to combine. Add the olive oil and shake again. Pour over the frisée and toss well. Add the golden bread cubes and bacon to the salad and toss. Serve on individual plates, each salad topped with a hot poached egg.

Artichokes with Vinaigrette Serves 6

Artichauts Vinaigrette is a dish for people who have plenty of time to eat it—and by the time you reach the tender hearts of the artichokes, I can guarantee that any ice between you and your dinner companions will have been well and truly broken!

6 globe artichokes, prepared as shown

For the vinaigrette
Juice of ½ lemon
2 teaspoons Dijon mustard
½ teaspoon sugar
Sea salt, to taste
Freshly ground black pepper, to taste
2 tablespoons white wine vinegar
6 tablespoons extra-virgin olive oil

Bring a large saucepan of lightly salted water to a boil. Put the artichokes in the boiling water, sit a colander on top of the pan to submerge them, and simmer for 30 to 40 minutes. The leaves should break away easily when the artichoke is cooked. Remove the artichokes and drain upside down to release all the water.

Meanwhile, make the vinaigrette: place the lemon juice, mustard, sugar, salt, and pepper in a jar with a tight-fitting lid and shake vigorously until blended. Add the vinegar and oil and shake vigorously until a smooth vinaigrette has formed.

If you know your friends like vinaigrette, pour it over the artichokes before serving. Alternatively, serve the vinaigrette in little dishes for dipping. Peel away the leaves and eat the soft kernel, pulling it off the leaf with your teeth. When you get to the artichoke bottom, in one firm tug pull away the hairy cluster (the choke) and discard it, and eat the sumptuous heart.

Fields of this majestic vegetable grow all over Brittany. Break the stalk away from the base, pulling any stringy bits with it. Use a sharp knife to cut the base flat, and peel away a few outer leaves. Plunge the artichokes into boiling water, cover, and cook for 30 to 40 minutes, until tender. Drain them upside down to get rid of excess water, then serve them whole, either dressed or with the vinaigrette on the side.

Basil and Arugula Salad with Melting Tomatoes   Serves 6

This is a lovely, simple salad in which the smoky flavor of the roasted tomatoes contrasts beautifully with the sweetness of the basil and the pepperiness of the arugula leaves.

Olive oil for roasting

½ pound cherry tomatoes
2 tablespoons extra-virgin olive oil
Juice of 1 lemon
1 teaspoon balsamic mustard
7 ounces fresh basil leaves
7 ounces fresh arugula, tough stems trimmed
Sea salt, to taste
Freshly ground black pepper, to taste

Heat the oven to 400°F.

Drizzle a little olive oil over a small roasting pan, add the tomatoes, and put in the oven to roast for 10 minutes, until they just begin to brown.

Put the extra-virgin olive oil in a salad bowl, add the lemon juice and balsamic mustard, and blend. Add the basil and arugula and toss until all the leaves are coated. Top with the hot tomatoes, sprinkle with sea salt and freshly ground black pepper, and serve at once.

Aïoli with Herbs   Serves 6

Use this versatile sauce as a dip for raw vegetables or as an accompaniment to grilled fish. Replace the herbs with a finely chopped chile to make a hot spicy sauce, great with bouillabaisse.

4 large egg yolks, at room temperature
1 tablespoon white wine vinegar
½ teaspoon dry mustard
6 garlic cloves, finely diced
Sea salt, to taste
Freshly ground black pepper, to taste
2 cups olive oil
Bunch of chives, finely chopped
Bunch of dill, finely chopped

Whisk together the yolks, 2 tablespoons water, the vinegar, and mustard using an electric hand-held mixer or a blender. (You have to work hard if you whisk by hand.) Add the garlic along with the salt and pepper, and blend again. Slowly pour in the olive oil, mixing constantly to emulsify the yolks and make a mayonnaise-style sauce. If the mixture is too thick, add a little extra water to adjust the consistency.

Stir the chopped chives and dill in well. Store in the refrigerator and use within 3 days.

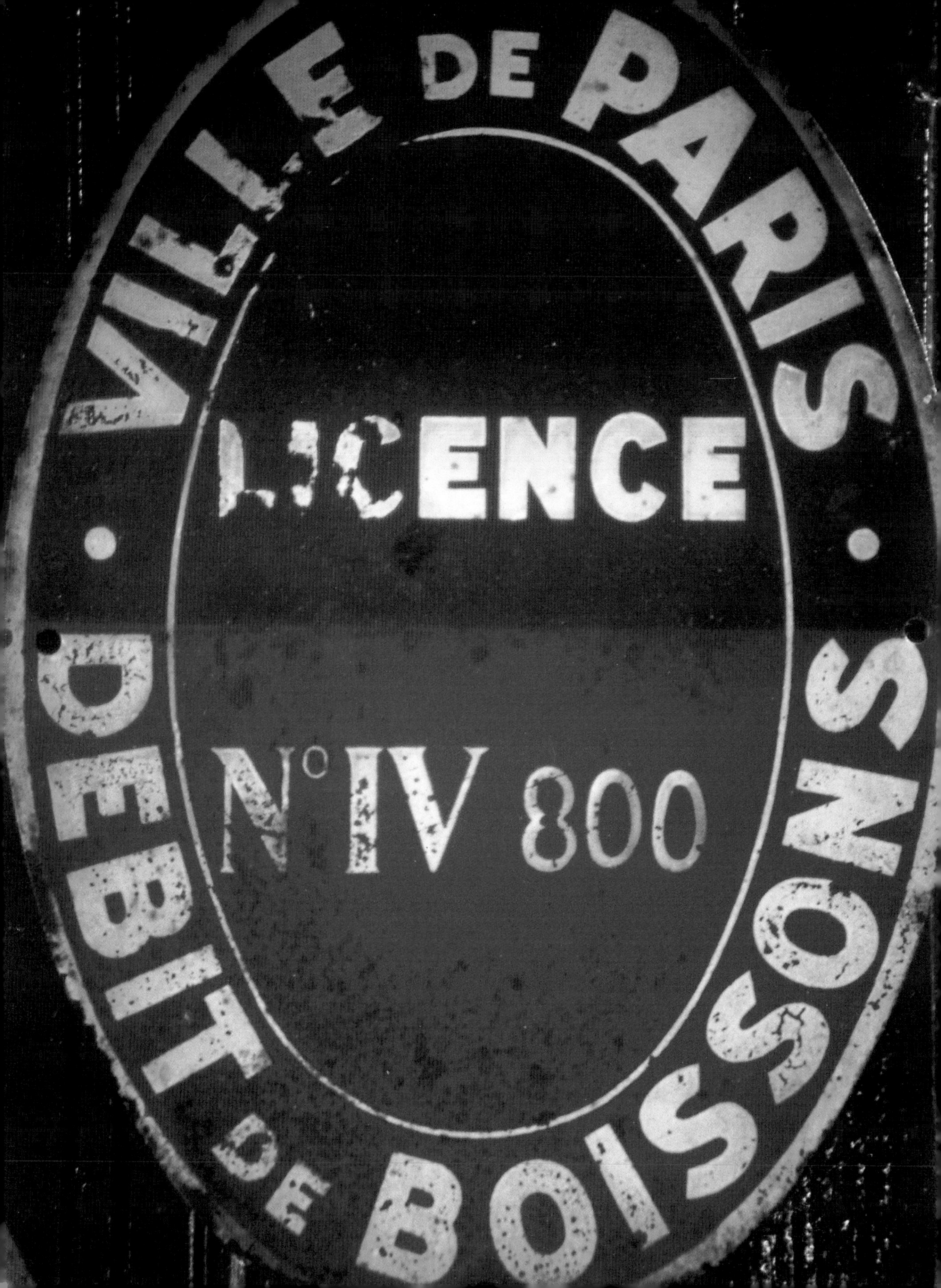
VILLE DE PARIS
LICENCE
N° IV 800
DEBIT DE BOISSONS

3 rue BACHAUM

Inc.ne Brasserie Auber

G de BAISSE de P

PLAT

DU JOUR 3

Service Rapide et Soi

Spécialité de Bouza

Soups & Starters

Originally, soups tended to be served at the beginning of the evening meal. There are many types, from clear consommés and bouillons, which are light and delicate, to the peasant stews like *pot-au-feu* or *poule au pot*, which are hearty enough to make up an entire meal.

I love making soups because they are so easy and versatile, and because of their comforting childhood associations, although a really elegant light soup is also a terrific way of starting a celebratory dinner.

Some of the starters in this chapter are adaptations of main courses that, depending on the occasion, can also be served in smaller portions as hors d'oeuvres. However, most French hors d'oeuvres are very simple, designed only to stimulate the appetite for the next course. Typically, try selections of any of the following:

Radishes served with fresh butter and sea salt

Tomatoes, sliced and salted, with chopped herbs and vinaigrette dressing

Marinated olives in oil

Half a melon, served with port

Grated carrots, tossed in oil, lemon, sea salt, and pepper

Charcuterie: a selection of pâté, sausage, smoked ham, and so on, served with pickled gherkins

The simplest meals are often the best. Try a rich, comforting homemade soup, served with lots of good bread—this is real fast food, good for all generations. Add a bottle of wine for the adults . . .

Don't be put off by the amount of garlic in this recipe.
Roasted garlic has a mellow, sweet flavor, a creamy
texture, and an irresistible aroma. Roast the garlic
cloves in their skins and then, when cool enough to
handle, squeeze the lovely flesh out. And once you've
conquered your garlic fears here, try Great-Aunt Simone's
Garlic Soup on page 40.

Gascony Tomato Soup   Serves 6

This rich, sweet soup—*Soupe de Tomates à la Gasconne*—relies on the traditional ingredients of Gascony for its powerful flavor. Serve with warm French bread.

1 pound cherry tomatoes
4 heads of garlic, cut in half crosswise
Olive oil as needed
Sea salt, to taste
Freshly ground black pepper, to taste
8 ounces mixed mushrooms, such as chanterelles,
    oysters, and/or stemmed shiitakes, sliced
1 red onion, diced
½ cup red wine
2 rosemary sprigs
1 bay leaf
1 quart vegetable stock
Bunch of flat-leaf parsley, chopped

Heat the oven to 300°F.

Put the tomatoes and halved garlic bulbs in a roasting pan with a little olive oil and the salt and pepper, toss well to coat in oil, then roast in the oven for 40 minutes. Remove from the oven and allow to cool.

Heat a drizzle of olive oil in a saucepan, add the mushrooms and red onion, and cook over medium heat for 5 minutes. Add the red wine, rosemary, bay leaf, and vegetable stock and gently simmer for 10 minutes.

When cool enough to handle, slip the garlic flesh out of its skin, then add it along with the tomatoes to the mushroom mix. Simmer gently for 1 hour—do not boil. Add the parsley just before serving.

Butternut Soup   Serves 6

This is a lovely way of using butternut squash, which has a sweet, subtle flavor and a meltingly tender consistency when properly cooked.

1 (3-pound) butternut squash
4 tablespoons (½ stick) unsalted butter
2 tablespoons olive oil, plus more to serve
2 onions, chopped
2 garlic cloves, chopped
1 teaspoon curry powder
Sea salt, to taste
Freshly ground black pepper, to taste
1½ quarts vegetable or chicken stock
Bunch of flat-leaf parsley, finely chopped

Butternuts are one of the hardest vegetables to cut. Always use a large sharp knife. The easiest way is to top and tail the butternut, then cut it crosswise in two. Stand each half on one end and cut away the skin from top to bottom. Halve each piece lengthways and remove the seeds.

Heat the butter and oil in a large saucepan, add the onions and garlic, and gently sauté until they soften. While the onions and garlic are sautéing, chop the butternut flesh, then add it to the onions and mix well. Stir in the curry powder, salt, and pepper. Pour in the stock, stir well, and bring to a boil. Simmer for 35 minutes, until the butternut is soft.

Blend the soup with an immersion blender (a worthwhile purchase, by the way, if you don't have one already). Serve topped with plenty of parsley and a drizzle of olive oil.

Onion Soup Serves 6

Subtle, smoky-flavored *Soupe à l'Oignon* is associated with the *réveillon* on Christmas Eve, and is a traditional winter favorite. Alexandre Dumas, in his *Grand Dictionnaire de la Cuisine,* tells the story of how King Stanislas, a noted gourmet, was served such a delicious onion soup while visiting his daughter and son-in-law in Versailles that he refused to leave without a demonstration of the recipe. Dumas describes the king in his dressing gown, a scarf around his head, tears running down his face as he watched the chef at work. Of course, this may just have been the onions . . .

3 tablespoons unsalted butter

1¾ pounds yellow onions, finely sliced
3 garlic cloves, chopped
2 tablespoons all-purpose flour
1½ quarts beef or vegetable stock
1 cup dry white wine
1 bay leaf
1 thyme sprig
Sea salt, to taste
Freshly ground black pepper, to taste
Bunch of curly parsley, finely chopped
½ baguette, cut into ¼-inch-thick slices
1 cup (4 ounces) finely shredded Gruyère cheese

Melt the butter in a large saucepan, add the onions, and cook over low heat for 50 minutes, stirring frequently. The onions should turn golden brown, be very soft, and begin to caramelize, which gives this soup its rich golden color and deep flavor.

Add the garlic along with the flour and mix well to allow the flour to absorb the excess butter, making a roux. Slowly pour in the stock and wine, stirring frequently, then bring to a gentle simmer. Add the bay leaf, thyme leaves (strip them from the sprig), salt, and pepper; cover with a lid and leave for 40 minutes over a low heat.

Five minutes before serving, add the parsley to the soup and stir well. Toast the slices of baguette and top with the Gruyère. Then broil the toast until the cheese is melted. Serve the soup in bowls topped with the cheesy toasts.

To me this bean soup smells of my grandmother's garden in spring. It is a wonderful way to make the most of young, homegrown vegetables if you are lucky enough to have them.

Bean Soup with *Pistou* Serves 6

This is a light and evocative dish, filled with the tastes, colors, and scents of approaching summer. It is extremely therapeutic to make, especially if you make the *pistou* by hand.

⅔ cup dried kidney beans
⅔ cup dried cannellini beans
1 tablespoon olive oil
1 onion, diced
2 celery stalks, finely chopped
2 potatoes, diced
1 leek, white and pale green part only, finely
    chopped
1 carrot, diced
1½ quarts vegetable or chicken stock
Sea salt, to taste
Freshly ground black pepper, to taste
4 tomatoes
5 ounces *haricots verts* or thin green beans, trimmed
1 zucchini
4 artichoke hearts
4 ounces vermicelli

For the pistou
6 garlic cloves, coarsely chopped
Generous bunch of basil
⅓ cup plus 1 tablespoon extra-virgin olive oil
Sea salt, to taste
Freshly ground black pepper, to taste

Soak the beans overnight in a saucepan of cold water. The next day, drain them, rinse well, and return to the pan. Cover with water, bring to a boil, and simmer for 1 hour. Skim off any froth that rises to the top during cooking. Drain and set aside.

To make the soup, heat the olive oil in a large saucepan and sauté the onion, celery, potatoes, leek, and carrot over medium-low heat for 20 minutes without browning them. Add the vegetable stock, cooked beans, salt, and pepper, and simmer for 20 minutes.

Meanwhile, score the skin of the tomatoes and plunge them into a pan of boiling water for 10 seconds, then remove and peel away the skin. Cut into quarters, remove the seeds, and dice the remaining flesh. Cut the green beans into 1-inch lengths, finely dice the zucchini, and slice the artichoke hearts into quarters. Add to the simmering soup along with the vermicelli and chopped tomatoes, and cook for 10 more minutes.

While the soup simmers, make the *pistou*—you can make it by hand in a mortar and pestle, or use a small blender. Combine the garlic and basil until they have almost formed a paste. Slowly mix in the olive oil, add the salt and pepper, and set aside.

Serve the soup with a spoonful of the *pistou* on top of each bowl.

Great-Aunt Simone's Garlic Soup   Serves 6

Soupe à l'Ail Simone Sorin is one of the great memory dishes of my childhood. During my summer holidays on Noirmoutier, my great-aunt Simone and great-uncle Jean would come to spend a few days with us. On her arrival, Simone, who is an enthusiastic cook, would often prepare this dish, one of her favorites. However far I had gone into the woods or along the beach, I could always tell when Great-Aunt Simone had arrived and was preparing her famous soup.

4 tablespoons olive oil
5 heads of garlic, cut in half crosswise
2 tablespoons all-purpose flour
1½ quarts hot water
4 thyme sprigs
Sea salt, to taste
Freshly ground black pepper, to taste
4 ounces vermicelli
Large bunch of flat-leaf parsley, finely chopped

Heat the oven to 275°F.

Drizzle the oil over a rimmed baking sheet and put the cut garlic bulbs on it. Roast for 1 to 1½ hours, until soft and golden.

Remove the garlic from the oven, and when cool enough to handle, squeeze out the soft, buttery flesh. Put it in a saucepan with the oil from the baking sheet and mash with a spoon. Over medium heat, mix in the flour so it absorbs the oil and makes a roux. Slowly pour in the hot water, stirring constantly. Add the thyme and salt and pepper, and simmer for 20 minutes.

Remove the saucepan from the heat, discard the thyme sprigs, and use an immersion blender to make the soup smooth (or puree in a regular blender). Return to the heat, add the vermicelli, and cook for 3 minutes. Add parsley just before serving.

Watercress Soup   Serves 6

Potage au Cresson is a lovely fresh, green soup, perfect for summer. It's also a great excuse to go out and buy those enormous bundles of watercress you find in farmers' markets.

2 tablespoons olive oil
1⅓ pounds potatoes, diced
1 small onion, chopped
10 ounces watercress, leaves and stems chopped
1 quart chicken or vegetable stock
Sea salt, to taste
Freshly ground black pepper, to taste
Pinch of freshly grated nutmeg

Heat the olive oil in a large pot and cook the potatoes and onion over medium-low heat for 20 minutes. Add the watercress (keep some leaves to use for garnish) and ⅓ cup water, and cook for 5 minutes, until the watercress wilts.

Add the stock, salt, pepper, and nutmeg; bring to a boil and gently simmer for 15 minutes.

Blend with an immersion blender until smooth (or puree in a regular blender). Check the seasoning, scatter with the reserved leaves, and serve at once.

This is an old-fashioned but versatile dish with as many variations as you can think of. Try it with *merguez* and a little couscous, or with smoked German sausage and sauerkraut to add a new twist.

Winter Sausage and Bean Soup Serves 6

Potage Haricots-Saucisses—the perfect comfort food for a miserable winter night.

1 pound dried cannellini beans
2 tablespoons olive oil
4 ounces slab bacon, cubed (see page 19)
2 onions, finely diced
2 carrots, finely diced
2 celery stalks, finely diced
2 garlic cloves, chopped
1 quart chicken stock
1 bay leaf
Sea salt, to taste
Freshly ground black pepper, to taste
3 spicy Toulouse sausages or 1 kielbasa
    (about 1 pound)
Bunch of flat-leaf parsley, chopped

Soak the beans overnight in a saucepan of cold water. The next day, drain them, rinse well, and return to the pan. Cover with water, bring to a boil, and simmer for 1 hour. Skim off any froth that rises to the top during cooking. Drain and set aside.

Heat the oil in a large saucepan and cook the bacon for 5 minutes, until golden. Add the onions, carrots, celery, and garlic, and gently sauté for 5 minutes. Pour in the stock, add the bay leaf, salt, and pepper, and stir. Add the sausages whole and simmer for 25 minutes with a lid on the pan.

Add the drained beans and simmer for 10 minutes. Remove the sausages, slice them, and return the slices to the pan. Sprinkle the soup with chopped parsley and serve.

There is only one way to chop garlic. Place the unpeeled clove on a chopping board. Take a large knife and, using the flat part of the blade under the heel of your hand, ruthlessly crush the garlic. Now you can easily peel it, chop it (as finely as you like), and put it in the pot.

You can still buy *galettes* from street vendors in most parts of Brittany, or you can make your own at home. They are good with *merguez* (red-looking, very spicy sausage made from beef, mutton, and red pepper), cheese, ham, or egg—or even simply with fresh butter—but for a special occasion try these *Galettes poireau-fromage*.

Buckwheat Crepes with Leek and Cheese Filling   Serves 6

Galettes de sarrazin, or buckwheat crepes, are the ultimate fast food. In my mother's hometown of Vitré, there is a stall that sells *galettes-saucisse* every market day, and one of my greatest treats was to buy them for lunch. They never made it to the table, though; ideally they should be eaten hot, out of a paper *cornet*, on a street corner or park bench.

For the crepes
1 cup buckwheat flour
1 cup all-purpose flour
1 cup milk (you can replace the milk with cider
     vinegar to make authentic crepes with a tangy
     flavor)
3 large eggs
Vegetable oil for the pan

For the filling
2 tablespoons olive oil
8 ounces slab bacon, cubed (see page 19)
5 large leeks, white and green parts only, sliced
2 garlic cloves, chopped
Sea salt, to taste
Freshly ground black pepper, to taste
1 cup (4 ounces) shredded Gruyère or Tomme de
     Savoie cheese
3 tablespoons crème fraîche
3 tablespoons unsalted butter, melted

First make the batter. Mix the buckwheat and all-purpose flours together in a large bowl, make a well in the center, add the milk, 1 cup of water, and the eggs and beat together until smooth. Allow to stand for 2 hours before cooking. If needed, stir in additional water to make a batter with the consistency of heavy cream.

Heat an 8-inch nonstick skillet or crepe pan and wipe very lightly with vegetable oil. Ladle in just enough batter to cover the bottom of the pan—tip the pan to make the mixture travel and coat the base evenly but lightly. Allow to set over medium heat, then flip with a metal spatula. Cook for another minute or so and then turn out. Repeat until all the batter is used. You should end up with about 18 crepes, even if you have had to throw the first one away. You can stack them with parchment paper between the layers.

Then make the filling. Heat the olive oil in a skillet over medium heat, add the bacon, leeks, and garlic, and cook for 10 minutes, stirring constantly. The aim is to cook the leeks until they are soft and any excess liquid has evaporated. Add the salt and pepper. Remove from the heat and stir in the Gruyère and crème fraîche.

Place a spoonful of the mixture on each crepe and fold into quarters to make little triangular cones.

Heat the oven to 375°F. Brush a baking sheet with some of the melted butter. Arrange the filled crepes on the baking sheet and brush with the remaining butter. Bake until the crepes are heated through, about 15 minutes. Serve at once.

Cheese Fondue Serves 6

Serve luxuriously rich and creamy *Fondue Franc-Comtoise* with a crisp green salad to clear the palate.

1 garlic clove, crushed
1½ pounds Gruyère or Beaufort cheese, grated
1 tablespoon cornstarch
1¼ cups white wine
Freshly ground black pepper, to taste
2 large baguettes, cut into cubes

Rub the inside of a heavy-bottomed saucepan with the crushed garlic clove. Toss the cheese with the cornstarch in a bowl.

Pour the wine into the garlic-scented pan and heat to boiling. Reduce the heat to low and add handfuls of the cheese, stirring until all the cheese is melted. Season with pepper. Serve the fondue at once, with cubes of bread for dipping.

Blue Cheese Bake Serves 6

The French name for this dish—*Soupe au Fromage*—is wonderfully misleading. It isn't a soup by modern standards; it is an old and very comforting baked cheese dish from the Auvergne region. It's very good as a main course, too, with a crisp green salad on the side.

Olive oil for sautéing and baking
4 red onions, diced
2 garlic cloves, chopped
1 cup dry white wine
1 cup chicken or vegetable stock
12 slices country-style bread
6 tomatoes, peeled
Bunch of basil
10 ounces St. Agur, Roquefort, or other blue cheese, sliced or crumbled
Sea salt, to taste
Freshly ground black pepper, to taste

Heat the oven to 400°F.

Heat a little olive oil in a skillet and gently sauté the onions and garlic for 10 minutes, until soft—do not brown or frizzle them. Add the white wine and stock, gently bring to a simmer, then remove from the heat.

Toast the slices of bread. Slice the tomatoes and roughly tear the basil. Rub a shallow baking dish with a little olive oil. Layer the dish with the toasted bread, sliced tomatoes, basil, all but ½ cup of the blue cheese, the salt, and pepper. Pour the onion mixture over the bread and top with the remaining ½ cup blue cheese. Bake for 15 minutes, then serve at once.

SALON DE THE

Pissaladière   Serves 6

I love the strong flavors of this dish, which combines two of my personal addictions: anchovies and olives. Use the best olives you can find—in the south of France there are olive markets that sell hundreds of differently spiced varieties—and those fat brown anchovies preserved in salt rather than oil.

For the onions
2 tablespoons olive oil
2 tablespoons unsalted butter
Bunch of thyme
3½ pounds yellow onions, very finely sliced
Sea salt, to taste
Freshly ground black pepper, to taste

For the dough
2 (¼-ounce) packages active dry yeast
⅔ cup lukewarm (105° to 115°F.) water
1 teaspoon sugar
2 cups unbleached flour
½ teaspoon sea salt
4 tablespoons olive oil, plus extra for brushing

12 salt-packed anchovies, rinsed (see page 23)
About 1 cup black Mediterranean olives, pitted

Prepare the onions. Warm 2 tablespoons of the olive oil and melt the butter in a large saucepan over low heat. Strip the thyme leaves from the stalks and add about half to the pan. Add the onions—it is important that the onions are very finely sliced—and cook over low heat for 1 hour, stirring occasionally; they should be soft and slightly caramelized but not brown. Season with salt and pepper and let cool.

Make the dough. Mix the yeast with the tepid water and sugar. Leave for 10 minutes in a warm place until the mixture becomes frothy.

Put the flour and salt in a mixing bowl, add the yeast mixture and olive oil, and mix until you have a dough ball. Lightly flour a work surface and knead the dough for 10 minutes, until the mixture is smooth and soft. Brush the inside of a bowl with a little olive oil, put the dough in, and cover with a cloth. Leave in a warm place to rise until the dough has doubled in size, about 1 hour.

Brush a rimmed baking sheet with a little olive oil.

Knock the air out of the dough on a lightly floured surface and knead for 2 minutes. Roll the dough out to a 12 × 10-inch rectangle, place on the baking sheet, and brush the surface of the dough with a little more olive oil. Cover with the cooked onions. Slice each anchovy into four long ribbons and arrange on top of the onions in a lattice pattern. Place the olives between the crisscrossed anchovies and sprinkle with the remaining thyme. Leave somewhere warm to rise again, uncovered, for 30 minutes.

Heat the oven to 425°F.

Bake the pissaladière for 20 to 25 minutes, and serve warm.

In southern France, slices of pissaladière wrapped in paper can be bought from a *boulangerie* and taken to the beach as a lunchtime snack. At home, serve thick slices of warm pissaladière with a green salad, or serve small squares of it with drinks.

The tastes in *Tarte Paysanne* vary according to the tomatoes you use. Ideally, use fresh, ripe, locally grown ones for the best flavor. Small, part-roasted cherry tomatoes work quite well, but my favorites are the big, shapeless Marmande tomatoes you can buy in French markets and which taste so good you might just want to eat them on their own . . .

Roasted Tomato Tart   Serves 6

Tarte Paysanne has a rich, sunny flavor. Make it with the best tomatoes you can find.

For the pastry
1½ cups all-purpose flour
5 tablespoons (½ stick plus 1 tablespoon) chilled unsalted butter, cut into small pieces
3 tablespoons chilled vegetable shortening, cut into small pieces
1 large egg, beaten

For the filling
3 tablespoons crème fraîche, or heavy cream whipped until lightly thickened
3 tablespoons Dijon mustard
10 to 12 large tomatoes, cored, peeled, and sliced
Sea salt, to taste
Freshly ground black pepper, to taste
4 fresh thyme sprigs
Olive oil for drizzling

Make the pastry. Put the flour in a large bowl, add the butter and shortening, and rub together with your fingertips until the mixture resembles bread crumbs. Using a round-bladed knife in a cutting motion, combine the egg with the mixture until a dough ball forms. Turn out onto a lightly floured surface and briefly knead until the dough is evenly mixed and smooth, then wrap and refrigerate for 30 minutes.

Heat the oven to 375°F.

Fill the tart. Roll out the dough on a lightly floured surface and line a 12-inch tart pan with a removable bottom. Mix the cream and mustard and spread over the pastry shell. Arrange the sliced tomatoes in the pastry, season with salt and pepper, and scatter thyme leaves—stripped from the stalks—over the top. Bake for 40 minutes. Drizzle with a little olive oil and serve warm or cold.

Quiche Lorraine   Serves 6

This is the original quiche, and once you have tasted the home-made variety you will never want to buy another one again. It is best served just warm (not hot) to bring out the creaminess of the filling and the contrast of textures.

For the pastry
1¾ cups all-purpose flour
5 tablespoons (½ stick plus 1 tablespoon) chilled unsalted butter, cut into small pieces
¼ cup chilled vegetable shortening, cut into small pieces
2 large egg yolks, lightly beaten with 2 tablespoons cold water

For the filling
Olive oil as needed
10 ounces slab bacon, cubed (see page 19)
2 large eggs
⅔ cup heavy cream
Sea salt, to taste
Freshly ground black pepper, to taste

Make the pastry. Put the flour in a large bowl, add the butter and shortening, and rub together with your fingertips until the mixture resembles bread crumbs. Using a round-bladed knife in a cutting motion, combine the beaten egg yolks with the mixture until a dough ball forms. Turn out onto a lightly floured surface and briefly knead until the dough is even and smooth, then wrap and refrigerate for 30 minutes.

Heat the oven to 375°F.

Roll out the dough on a lightly floured surface and line a 12-inch tart pan with a removable bottom. Heat a little olive oil in a skillet and cook the bacon for 5 minutes. In a bowl, beat the eggs, cream, salt, and pepper until blended, then add the bacon. Pour into the pastry case. Bake for 35 minutes, reduce the temperature to 325°F., and bake for 15 minutes more. Serve warm.

Peeled tomatoes take on a whole, new velvety texture.
Once you start peeling tomatoes for your recipes, you
won't look back. Make a cross in the bottom of each one,
plunge into boiling water for 10 seconds (a little more if
the tomatoes are not fully ripe), remove, and peel. It's
that simple.

Onion Tart   Serves 6

Beautifully smoky-sweet and delicate, *Tarte à l'oignon* is perfect as a main course with a summer salad, or as an autumn starter.

For the pastry
1¾ cups all-purpose flour
12 tablespoons (1½ sticks) chilled unsalted butter,
    cut into small pieces
2 large egg yolks, lightly beaten
Dried beans for baking the shell

For the filling
3 tablespoons unsalted butter
2 tablespoons olive oil
1 pound yellow onions, finely sliced
⅔ cup half-and-half or light cream
2 large eggs
½ teaspoon freshly grated nutmeg
Sea salt, to taste
Freshly ground black pepper, to taste

Make the pastry. Put the flour in a large bowl, add the butter, and rub together with your fingertips until the mixture resembles bread crumbs. Using a round-bladed knife in a cutting motion, combine the egg yolks with the mix until a dough ball forms. Turn out onto a lightly floured surface and briefly knead until the dough is even and smooth, then wrap and refrigerate to chill for 30 minutes.

Heat the oven to 400°F.

Roll out the pastry on a lightly floured surface and line a 12-inch tart pan with a removable bottom, making sure there are no cracks. Return to the refrigerator to chill for another 20 minutes, then line with parchment paper and fill with the dried beans. Bake for 20 minutes, reduce the heat to 325°F., and bake for about 15 minutes more, or until the pastry is golden and set. Remove from the oven.

While the pastry is baking, make the filling. Melt the butter with the oil in a saucepan. Add the onions and cook over low heat for 30 minutes. This long, slow method of cooking makes the onions melt; do not allow them to brown or frizzle.

Mix the cream, eggs, nutmeg, salt, and pepper in a bowl. Put the cooked onions in the baked pastry shell, carefully pour in the egg mixture, and then return the tart to the oven to cook for 25 to 30 minutes. Serve warm or cold.

Tartelette Méridionale   Serves 6

A terrific summer dish, lush with the flavors of southern France, as its name suggests . . .

For the pastry
1½ cups all-purpose flour
6 tablespoons (¾ stick) chilled unsalted butter, cut into small pieces
2 tablespoons chilled vegetable shortening, cut into small pieces
1 large egg, beaten
Dried beans for baking the shell

For the filling
Olive oil as needed
50 cherry tomatoes, halved
1 garlic clove, chopped
About 3 tablespoons tapenade, store-bought or homemade
6 salted anchovy fillets (see page 23)
Bunch of fresh basil
1 cup black Mediterranean olives, pitted
Sea salt, to taste
Freshly ground black pepper, to taste

Make the pastry. Put the flour in a large bowl, add the butter and shortening, and rub together with your fingertips until the mixture resembles bread crumbs. Using a round-bladed knife in a cutting motion, combine the egg with the mix until a dough ball forms. Turn out onto a lightly floured surface and briefly knead until the dough is even and smooth, then wrap and place in the refrigerator to chill for 30 minutes.

Heat the oven to 375°F.

Roll out the dough pastry on a lightly floured surface and line six 4-inch tartelette pans with removable bottoms. Line each pan with parchment paper, cover with a layer of dried beans, and bake for 25 minutes. Take out of the oven, remove the beans and parchment, and set the shells aside. Reduce the temperature to 250°F.

Pour a little oil in a roasting pan, add the tomatoes and garlic, and toss well. Roast in the oven for 1 hour.

Roughly spread about a teaspoon of the tapenade over the base of each pastry shell. Top with one anchovy fillet, a few basil leaves, the roasted tomatoes, and a few olives. Drizzle with olive oil—you could use what's left in the roasting pan—season with salt and pepper, and cook for 10 minutes more. Serve at room temperature.

Tapenade   Serves 6

This is what I eat when I've had too much chocolate. It's lovely to make by hand with a mortar and pestle, which really brings out the aroma of the ingredients. It's versatile, too; you can serve it with good bread, as a dip with crudités, or tossed over warm pasta; and if you add a little extra oil to the mixture, it makes an excellent dressing for celery or lettuce hearts.

You can make tapenade in advance and it will last in the refrigerator for up to four days (if you can resist it!). Add chile for a change if you like.

10 ounces pitted black or green Mediterranean olives
8 salted anchovy fillets (see page 23)
3 tablespoons salted capers, rinsed of their salt, or use drained bottled capers
1 garlic clove
Juice of ½ lemon
Sea salt, to taste
Freshly ground black pepper, to taste
¾ cup extra-virgin olive oil

Put all the ingredients except the oil in a mortar or a blender and pound or blend to a rough chop. Slowly pour in the olive oil and combine to form a paste. Store in the refrigerator.

Chile Garlic Bread is my daughter's favorite recipe: she loves both the making and the eating of it. It's easy enough for her to prepare without too much help while at the same time allowing her to create plenty of enjoyable mess.

Anouchka's Chile Garlic Bread   Serves 6

My daughter's favorite recipe. If the strength of the garlic seems a little overpowering to you, roast it in the oven for a sweeter, more delicate taste before blending it with the other ingredients in a mortar and pestle. Don't use a blender—half the fun of this very simple recipe is mixing it by hand and getting messy! Do take care, though, with little people's eyes and skin, or it could all end in tears: make sure children of all ages wash their hands after touching the chile.

1 medium-hot fresh red chile, such as jalapeño or red cherry
4 garlic cloves, chopped
1 thyme sprig
1 teaspoon coarse sea salt
12 tablespoons (1½ sticks) unsalted butter, softened
1 baguette

Heat the oven to 375°F.

Cut the chile in half lengthways, remove the seeds, and dice the flesh. (Keep the seeds in if you like the heat.) Put the chile, garlic, thyme leaves (stripped from the stalks), and salt in a mortar and pestle, and pound until it forms a paste. Put the butter in a bowl, add the paste, and mix well.

Slice the bread almost to the bottom every 1¼ inches or so, then put some of the butter into each incision, spreading it over the inner surfaces. Put the bread on a baking sheet and bake for 8 to 10 minutes. Serve hot.

Joe's Potato Bread   Serves 6

This is not a true bread as we are used to it. It is denser because of the potato, and contains no yeast. It will rise only marginally at room temperature—don't expect miracles. But it makes a dense and comforting bread, perfect with soup on a chilly winter's day.

12 ounces baking potatoes, such as russets or Burbanks, scrubbed but unpeeled
6 tablespoons unsalted butter, melted
2 large egg yolks
Bunch of flat-leafed parsley
2¼ cups self-rising flour (not self-rising cake flour)
⅓ cup raisins
3 tablespoons sunflower seeds
2 tablespoons milk
¼ teaspoon sea salt
1 large egg, beaten, for glazing the bread

Heat the oven to 400°F.

Pierce the potatoes several times with a knife and bake for about 40 minutes, until tender. Set the potatoes aside until cool enough to handle, then cut them in half and scoop the flesh into a bowl. Mash and set aside to cool completely.

Add the butter, egg yolks, and parsley to the cooled potato, and blend well. Then add the flour, raisins, sunflower seeds, milk, and salt, and mix well again until it forms a dough ball.

Lightly flour a work surface and knead the dough for 5 minutes, until smooth. Cover and leave in a warm place for 35 minutes.

Knead the bread again for 5 minutes. Butter a 8½ × 4½-inch loaf pan. Shape the bread to fit the pan, cover, and let stand for 35 minutes in a warm place.

Heat the oven to 375°F.

Brush the top of the loaf all over with the beaten egg, then bake it for 40 minutes. Serve warm, and eat on the same day as baking.

Three-Mushroom Vol-au-Vents Serves 6

Vol-au-vent means "blown on the wind," and these little pastries should be almost as light as air.

For the puff pastry

1⅓ cups all-purpose flour
2 tablespoons chilled vegetable shortening, cut into small pieces
12 tablespoons (1½ sticks) chilled unsalted butter, cut into small pieces
⅓ cup ice-cold water
1 large egg, beaten, for glazing

For the filling

1 tablespoon olive oil
6 ounces stemmed shiitake mushrooms, roughly chopped
6 ounces chanterelle mushrooms, roughly chopped
6 ounces button mushrooms, roughly chopped
2 shallots, diced
½ cup heavy cream
1 tablespoon grainy mustard, such as Meaux
1 tablespoon cognac
Sea salt, to taste
Freshly ground black pepper, to taste

Make the pastry. Put the flour in a large bowl, add the shortening and butter, and rub together with your fingertips until the mixture resembles bread crumbs. Add the cold water, mixing it in with a round-bladed knife until a dough ball forms. Turn out onto a lightly floured surface and briefly knead the dough until even and smooth, then wrap and chill for 30 minutes.

Lightly dust a cool work surface with flour and roll the dough out to approximately 5 × 9 inches. Dot a little butter over the dough. Fold one-third of the pastry over toward the center, then fold the remaining single layer over to make three layers (like a thick folded business letter). Press the edges together to stop the butter from escaping. Turn the dough 90 degrees, lightly dust, and roll it out once more to the above size. Again, turn the pastry 90 degrees, fold into thirds, and press the edges together. Roll out and repeat one more time. Wrap and refrigerate to chill and relax for 30 minutes. Remove the dough and repeat the above (roll out and fold into thirds three more times), then chill for another 30 minutes. Then repeat the whole process (roll and fold into thirds three more times for a total of nine times). You could buy frozen puff pastry patty shells, but this is more fun, and the result is better.

Heat the oven to 425°F.

Roll out the pastry to a scant ¼-inch thickness and cut out 12 small or 6 large rounds with a pastry cutter. Place them on a water-dampened baking sheet and return to the refrigerator to chill for 30 minutes. Take a cutter half the size of your first one and cut an indentation in the center of each pastry circle, being careful not to cut all the way through to the baking sheet. Take a small knife and knock up all around the edges of the vol-au-vent shells to help the pastry to rise in crispy layers.

Brush the top of each shell with the beaten egg, making sure no egg goes down the sides or it will glue the layers together and undo the effect of your knocking up. Bake for 30 minutes.

While the cases are baking, make the filling: Heat the olive oil in a skillet, add the mushrooms and shallots, and cook over medium-high heat, stirring constantly. If there are a lot of juices in the pan, increase the heat and cook until they reduce. Remove six good-looking mushroom slices (any variety) for garnish, and keep them warm. Add the cream, mustard, cognac, and salt and pepper, and simmer for 5 minutes, stirring constantly.

After the pastry shells have been in the oven for 30 minutes, take them out and lift out the center of each pastry case, putting it to one side. Return the tray to the oven and cook for 3 more minutes, then fill with the mushroom mixture, top with the reserved mushrooms and the pastry caps, and serve.

Even children who won't eat cabbage should enjoy this tasty, hearty dish. As a child it took me a long time to realize that this firm, delicious green leaf and the anemic white stuff I was given at school were one and the same ingredient . . .

Cabbage Galette   Serves 6

This is an old peasant dish from the Auvergne region, and although it is known as *Galette au Chou*, it is quite different from the thin Breton *galettes*. It is dense and filling, and can be eaten hot or cold, although I think this dish is best served just warm.

½ head green cabbage, preferably Savoy, cored and
 roughly chopped
2 tablespoons olive oil
7 ounces slab bacon, cubed (see page 19)
2 large eggs
3 shallots, finely diced
Bunch of flat-leaf parsley, finely chopped
3 garlic cloves, chopped
Sea salt, to taste
Freshly ground black pepper, to taste
1 cup milk
1½ cups all-purpose flour

Heat the oven to 350°F.

Steam the cabbage for 3 minutes over boiling water. Smear a pie dish with olive oil and heat it in the oven.

In a large bowl, mix the bacon, eggs, shallots, parsley, garlic, salt, and pepper. Add the milk and flour, and mix into a smooth dough.

Remove the hot pie dish from the oven. Spread half the dough over the base of the dish, pile on the cabbage and pack it down with your hands, and cover with the remaining dough. Bake for 35 minutes, until golden and firm.

Fish

My favorite fish recipe begins like this: "Take a boat, a fishing rod, a frying pan and a jar of mustard. . . ." Many people avoid cooking fish because they think it will be difficult, but fish recipes can be as easy or as complicated as you want to make them. The essential thing is that your fish should be absolutely fresh. During my childhood I spent my holidays with my uncle Paul, who was a fisherman, and there was always a plentiful supply of freshly caught local fish. This is the ideal situation, but failing that, it's a good idea to befriend an approachable fishmonger who can advise you and who will prepare your fish for you on the spot (ready-filleted fish loses its taste rapidly). All along the French coast you can find terrific fish markets, and in many harbors you can buy fresh-caught shellfish, crabs, and lobsters from the fishermen themselves. It is wonderful holiday food because most fish and shellfish are very quick and simple to prepare and to cook, even on a portable stove or barbecue.

Don't be nervous about using mussels, clams, and other shellfish. Just make sure they are very fresh—if you buy them from a fish shop, make sure it's a busy one with a fast turnover. The shells should be closed. Sometimes the low temperature of the refrigerator acts as an anesthetic and the shells open; just bang them on a hard surface and slowly they should shut; if not, discard them. Wash them well in a large sink of cold running water. Use a small knife to rip away the stringy beard around the lip of mussels. Discard any damaged shells, and any shells that do not open when cooked.

One of the great pleasures of the French coast is going into a café and ordering fresh seafood and one of the dry, cheerful local wines. Muscadet or Gros-Plant makes an excellent accompaniment, though a rosé (such as an Anjou) gives a more fragrant, flowery taste. Serve very cold.

Moules Marinière   Serves 6

I first tasted this dish when I was six years old. Like many small children, I was reluctant to eat shellfish at first, but on this occasion my mother persuaded me to taste hers. Unfortunately for my mother, I not only tasted her dish but also finished the lot, and I have loved mussels ever since. On Noirmoutier I used to collect them from the rocks in front of the house, pick the bay leaves off the tree in the next-door neighbor's garden, dig for garlic in the dunes where it grew wild, and cook the whole lot in sea water, which my mother insists is the key ingredient. Serve with warm crusty bread and a green salad.

4 tablespoons (½ stick) unsalted butter
2 tablespoons olive oil
2 garlic cloves, finely diced
1 onion, finely diced
3 pounds mussels, cleaned and washed (see page 68)
¾ cup dry white wine (Muscadet works well)
1 bay leaf
Sea salt, to taste
Freshly ground black pepper, to taste
Large bunch of flat-leaf parsley, chopped

Gently heat the butter and olive oil in a large saucepan, add the garlic and onion, and sauté for 5 minutes—do not brown or frizzle them. Then add the mussels, wine, bay leaf, salt, and pepper, bring to a boil, cover, and cook for 10 minutes, or until all the mussel shells have opened. Finally, add the parsley, put the lid back on, and shake vigorously. Serve at once.

Georges Payen's Razor Clams
Serves 6

This is a quick and delicious way of serving razor clams—*couteaux*—with garlic and chile, perfect for a warm summer night on the beach. At my grandfather's house you could catch the clams—if you were very patient and quiet—when the tide was out. And finding and catching these shellfish was one of my favorite pastimes as a child, although it took me a long time to enjoy eating the clams themselves! These elusive creatures live deep in the sand and come out only when the tide is high. You have to sprinkle salt around the clam's hole to fool it into believing the tide has come in, then, when it pops out—only for a split second—you have to grab it very fast, or it disappears again for good. In those days before computer games, it was a great exercise in hand-eye coordination. Now, of course, you can buy razor clams from a well-stocked fishmonger, which is less time-consuming (but much less fun). Serve with lots of warm bread to mop up the cooking juices.

2 tablespoons unsalted butter
Dash of olive oil
24 razor clams
2 garlic cloves, finely diced
1 hot red chile, seeded and finely diced
½ cup dry white wine
Bunch of flat-leaf parsley, chopped
Freshly ground black pepper, to taste

Heat the butter and olive oil in a large skillet, add the razor clams, garlic, and chile, and cook for 5 minutes. Pour in the white wine, place a lid on the pan, and cook rapidly for another 5 minutes. Finally, add the parsley and pepper, toss, and serve at once.

Noirmoutier Oysters Serves 6

Some recipes use cooked oysters, but much more usual is to eat them raw, with nothing but a little lemon juice or shallot vinegar, a glass of Muscadet, and a view of the ocean.

2 shallots, very finely diced
3 tablespoons red wine vinegar
24 large oysters
Seaweed or crushed ice, to garnish

For serving
1 lemon, cut into wedges
Sourdough bread, finely sliced
Hot red pepper sauce
Freshly ground black pepper

Mix the shallots and vinegar in a small bowl. To shuck the oysters, place each oyster, rounded side down, in a cloth and hold with one hand. Insert the tip of an oyster knife at the narrow end of the oyster, between the two shells, and wiggle, keeping the blade flat. You may need some strength, but the shell will eventually give and open. Run the knife along the inside of the top shell to release the oyster muscle, remove the top shell, and cut the oyster free from the bottom shell.

Arrange the prepared oysters on a bed of crushed ice or seaweed. Serve with the shallot vinegar, lemon wedges, sourdough bread, a bottle of hot red pepper sauce, and the peppermill at the table.

The coast of Brittany and the Vendée is traditionally oyster *(huître)* country. Cancale oysters are particularly good, but you can find oysters all the way down the coast.

Seafood Platter   Serves 6

If I were to plan my last meal, Fruits de Mer would be the main course. To me it evokes everything that is good about food: the joy of excellent ingredients, simply presented; the time it takes to eat; and the pleasure of eating in an informal environment, surrounded by friends and family. This is not a dish to be consumed in haste, or in silence, or in pretentious or intimidating surroundings, or in uncongenial company. It requires time and leisure. It encourages conversation, cooperation, intimacy, and friendship. It is the ideal thing for a large and cheery get together—and even better for a candlelit dinner for two, with lots of chilled champagne.

12 Littleneck clams
12 langoustines (see Note)
3 large crabs, such as Dungeness
1 pound large shrimp (size according to budget!)
12 mussels
12 whelks (see Note)
12 periwinkles (see Note)
Seaweed or crushed ice, to serve
12 large oysters

For serving
3 lemons, cut in half
Red wine shallot vinegar (see Noirmoutier Oysters, page 72)
Hot red pepper sauce
Hearty, dense country bread, thinly sliced

Note: Langoustines, whelks, and periwinkles are available at well-stocked fish markets serving an ethnic clientele. If unavailable, delete them and substitute additional clams, shrimp, mussels, and oysters.

Reserve all your cooking water as you go, and freeze it for a fish stew or soup. Here goes.

Clams: purge them by soaking them in a large bowl of water and then draining and repeating the soaking until no more sand comes out of them.

Langoustines: plunge them into a saucepan of lightly salted boiling water and simmer for 5 minutes, then drain and chill them.

Crabs: plunge them into a large pot of lightly salted boiling water and simmer for 6 minutes per pound, then drain and chill them. Separate the central part of the underbody from the shell with your hands or a knife. Remove and discard the soft gray feather gills. Cut each crab in half vertically.

Shrimp: plunge them into a saucepan of lightly salted boiling water and simmer for 3 to 5 minutes. Drain and chill them.

Mussels: heat a scant amount of water in a pan with a little knob of butter, add the cleaned mussels (see page 68), place the lid on, and simmer for 5 minutes.

Whelks: plunge them into a saucepan of lightly boiling water and simmer for 10 minutes, then drain and chill them.

Periwinkles: plunge them into a saucepan of lightly salted boiling water and simmer for 5 minutes, then drain and chill them.

To serve, cover a huge platter with seaweed or crushed ice. Open the oysters with an oyster knife (see page 72) and place them together on the platter. Using a clam knife, open the clams and cluster them together. Arrange the langoustines, shrimp, whelks, and periwinkles all together. Place the mussels in a bowl on the platter. Crown the seafood with the cooked crabs and then garnish with lemon halves. Serve with a dish of shallot vinegar, a bottle of red pepper sauce, and a basket of sliced bread. Eat at once with finger bowls and large napkins on the side.

Jean Sorin's Fisherman's Stew   Serves 6

Soupe du Pêcheur is an extrovert, a sociable dish impossible to eat without a certain amount of mess. It is excellent comfort food for the evening after a long, cold day's fishing, with a loaf of really good country bread.

3 tablespoons olive oil
3 onions, chopped
3 garlic cloves, chopped
2 hot red chiles, seeded and chopped
Pinch of saffron
Sea salt, to taste
Freshly ground black pepper, to taste
2 (14½-ounce) cans chopped tomatoes in juice
1⅓ cups dry white wine
1 tablespoon tomato paste
1¼ pounds small red-skinned potatoes
1 pound mixed, cleaned shellfish: mussels, shrimp, scallops, or clams
2 pounds fish fillets: any combination of snapper, halibut, sea bass, haddock, tuna, swordfish, and/or marlin
Large bunch of flat-leaf parsley, finely chopped

Heat the olive oil in a large saucepan. Add the onions, garlic, chiles, saffron, salt, and pepper and soften over gentle heat for 10 minutes. Add the chopped tomatoes with their juices, wine, and tomato paste. Bring to a boil and cook for 5 minutes to reduce some of the liquid.

Add the potatoes and simmer gently for 15 minutes.

Add the shellfish and then carefully lay the fish fillets on top. Cover with a lid and simmer for 10 minutes, until the fillets are opaque when lightly prodded apart with the tip of a knife.

Just before serving, add lots of chopped parsley. Serve in large, wide soup bowls, with plenty of finger bowls at the table.

My great-uncle Jean taught me this dish, but it
is best not to rely entirely on one's own fishing to provide
all the ingredients. I always allow for a visit to the local
fish market before I begin . . .

Rich Bouillabaisse Serves 6

This very old recipe was originally cooked in a pot balanced on three stones, and was a dish of the poor, designed to make the most of cheap, common ingredients. It is almost impossible to make authentic bouillabaisse other than in the south of France because the rascasse and other Mediterranean rock fish that are traditionally used in its making are just not available elsewhere. This "rich" version—*Bouillabaisse riche*—uses monkfish instead, but you can adapt the recipe to any kind of fish or shellfish. In Marseilles, the *bouillon* is served with a local bread called *marette*, with the fish on the side. The legend goes that the goddess Venus first made it for her husband, Vulcan, to send him to sleep while she disported herself elsewhere. Serve bouillabaisse with lots of warm French bread, and try it with a spoonful of chile aïoli, a variation of the herb aïoli on page 29.

4 tablespoons olive oil
2 onions, diced
1 fennel bulb, trimmed and diced
2 leeks, white and pale green parts only, trimmed
    and finely sliced
3 celery stalks, finely sliced
2 garlic cloves, diced
1 tablespoon all-purpose flour
2 (14½-ounce) cans chopped tomatoes in juice
1 thyme sprig
Pinch of saffron
2 bay leaves
1 quart fish stock
1½ pounds monkfish, trimmed and cut into
    6 portions
6 sea scallops
6 large shrimp, peeled and deveined
Sea salt, to taste
Freshly ground black pepper, to taste
Large bunch of chives, finely chopped

Heat the olive oil in a large saucepan. Add the onions, fennel, leeks, celery, and garlic and sauté over medium heat for 10 minutes, stirring frequently—do not allow them to brown.

Sprinkle in the flour and blend well to absorb any excess oil, then add the tomatoes, thyme, saffron, and bay leaves and mix well. Pour in the fish stock, bring to a boil, then reduce the heat and simmer for 15 minutes.

Add the monkfish, scallops, shrimp, salt, and pepper; cover with a lid and simmer very gently for 10 minutes.

Just before serving, add the chives. Serve the bouillabaisse in large soup bowls.

Salmon in Parchment Paper
Serves 6

This is an excellent way to cook fish so that it stays tender and moist, with a light, delicate flavor. Its French name is *Saumon en Papillote*.

5 celery stalks, sliced
4 shallots, sliced
Bunch of flat-leaf parsley, chopped
Sea salt, to taste
Freshly ground black pepper, to taste
6 (5- to 6-ounce) skinless salmon fillets
1 lemon, cut into 6 wedges

Heat the oven to 400°F. Cut six 10-inch rounds out of baking parchment.

Put the celery and shallots in a bowl, add the parsley, salt, and pepper and mix well.

Arrange the paper rounds on the work surface. Place equal amounts of the vegetable mixture in the center of each paper and top with a salmon fillet and a wedge of lemon. Close up each parcel, securing the contents by twisting the paper above the fish like an old-fashioned purse. Place on a baking sheet and bake for 15 minutes. Serve in the paper parcels, but take care when opening, as hot steam may rush out.

Salmon in Red Wine
Serves 6

This unusual combination—*Saumon au Vin Rouge*—makes for a rich, earthy dish, excellent with pasta (serve it, for example, on piles of fettuccine) or rice.

3 tablespoons unsalted butter
1 tablespoon olive oil
1 red onion, chopped
4 ounces mushrooms, sliced
1 garlic clove, chopped
3 tablespoons all-purpose flour
1 (750-milliliter) bottle red Burgundy or Pinot Noir
Sea salt, to taste
Freshly ground black pepper, to taste
6 (5- to 6-ounce) salmon fillets, with skin left on

Melt the butter with the olive oil in a big, wide saucepan; add the onion, mushrooms, and garlic and sauté gently for 10 minutes.

Sprinkle in the flour and mix well until it has absorbed the oil and butter, then gradually add the red wine and mix until smooth. Season with salt and pepper, and bring to a boil. Add the salmon fillets and spoon the red wine over them to stain them evenly. Cover, then simmer gently for 8 minutes.

Lift out the salmon and keep warm. Bring the wine back to a boil, mix well, then with a slotted spoon, lift out all the mushrooms and serve them with the salmon.

Don't discard the poaching liquid—it can be stored in the freezer and reused.

A light, fresh dish for a summer by the sea, this Breton recipe, Skate with Caper-Herb Butter, makes the most of the delicate consistency of the skate, with the tangy capers an ideal contrast to the fish's rather sweet flesh.

Skate with Caper-Herb Butter   Serves 6

This is delicious with the Mashed Potatoes with Nutmeg (page 167). Use salt-preserved anchovies, if you can.

Bunch of watercress
Bunch of flat-leaf parsley
Bunch of chervil
Bunch of tarragon
Bunch of chives
3 tablespoons salt-packed capers, rinsed of salt, or use
    drained and rinsed bottled capers
3 anchovy fillets, preferably salt-preserved
    (see page 23)
1 garlic clove
1 cup (2 sticks) unsalted butter, at room temperature
Juice of ½ lemon
Freshly ground black pepper, to taste
6 (5- to 6-ounce) portions of skate

Heat the oven to 400°F.

Trim the stems of the watercress, parsley, chervil, and tarragon. Put the herb leaves, chives, capers, anchovies, and garlic in a mini food processor and blend until finely chopped. (You could do this by hand, but you would need a little patience.) Add the butter, lemon juice, and pepper and blend until evenly mixed. Scoop out and place in a serving bowl.

Heat a large, lightly oiled jelly-roll pan in the oven for 5 minutes.

Pat the skate dry with paper towels to remove excess moisture, then place on the heated pan. Drizzle with a little olive oil and roast in the top third of the oven for 15 minutes. Serve immediately with scoops of the soft herb butter on top of each portion of skate.

Trout with Fennel Serves 6

Fennel gives a spicy anise flavor to this rich and creamy dish, *Truite au Fenouil*.

6 rainbow or brook trout, cleaned
Olive oil
3 fennel bulbs, trimmed, cored, and finely sliced
1½ cups (6 ounces) freshly grated Parmesan
Sea salt, to taste
Freshly ground black pepper, to taste
⅓ cup heavy cream
⅓ cup dry white wine

Heat the oven to 350°F. Rinse the trout under cold water and dry with paper towels. Place on a large, lightly oiled baking sheet.

Lightly oil a large baking dish and layer the fennel with half of the Parmesan, seasoning each layer with salt and pepper. Pour the cream and white wine over the top, and sprinkle with the remaining Parmesan.

Cover the fennel dish with aluminum foil and bake for 20 minutes, then remove the foil and bake for 10 minutes. Add the fish to the fennel and bake for 20 minutes. Serve the fish on a bed of fennel.

Normandy Trout Serves 6

Truite au Trou Normand is a simple dish that takes on another dimension when the flambéed Calvados is poured over just before serving.

6 rainbow or brook trout, cleaned
8 tablespoons (1 stick) unsalted butter
Sea salt, to taste
Freshly ground black pepper, to taste
⅓ cup Calvados

Heat the oven to 275°F.

Rinse the trout under cold water and dry with paper towels. Melt 4 tablespoons of the butter over medium heat in a large skillet. Add three trout, and cook on each side for 6 minutes.

Place in an ovenproof serving dish and keep warm in the oven while you melt the remaining butter and cook the other trout in the same way. Add them to the serving dish and season with salt and pepper.

Heat the Calvados in a small saucepan over low heat. Ignite carefully with a long match, and let the flame burn for a few seconds, then cover with a lid to extinguish the flame. Pour the Calvados over the trout and serve at once.

Pike with Butter Sauce   Serves 6

The Loire is a long, murky, and dangerous river, broad enough to have sandy islets along some parts of its length and endlessly fascinating to children. It is there, with my friends Eric and Pilou Imbach, that I learned to build rafts out of river debris, to dive under the submerged tree roots (swimming in the Loire was absolutely forbidden, which is why I did it), and to fish for pike. The fish were virtually inedible, half bones and half sewage, and my mother was obliged to find all kinds of ingenious ways of "forgetting" our catch when it was time for me to go home. All the same, it was terrific fun and has left me with a fondness for this fish.

1 whole pike, or another fish with firm white flesh (approximately 4 pounds)

For the court-bouillon
3 quarts water
1 bottle dry white wine
2 carrots, chopped
2 onions, chopped
2 celery stalks, chopped
2 garlic cloves, chopped
2 thyme sprigs
2 bay leaves
Bunch of flat-leaf parsley
1 tablespoon sea salt
1 teaspoon whole black peppercorns
Pinch of fennel seeds

For the beurre blanc
2 shallots, diced
Juice of ½ lemon
1 pound unsalted butter, at room temperature, cut in pieces
Sprigs of flat-leaf parsley to garnish

Gut and clean the pike well under running cold water, and cut off the fins and tail, and, if you must, the head. (You can always ask your fishmonger to do this.)

Place the court-bouillon ingredients in a large poaching pan or oval roasting pan, cover with a lid, and bring to a boil, then simmer for 25 minutes.

Carefully add the pike to the court-bouillon, bring back to a very gentle simmer, and cook for 30 minutes. Remove the pan from the heat, remove 1 cup of the liquid, and allow the fish to rest in the remaining court-bouillon while you make the *beurre blanc*.

Boil the 1 cup court-bouillon, the shallots, and lemon juice in a nonreactive skillet until reduced by half. Reduce the heat to low. Whisking constantly, add small pieces of butter until all is absorbed and you have a creamy sauce. Do not boil. Remove from the heat.

Lift the pike out of the poaching pan, drain, and garnish with the parsley. Serve the sauce separately.

Pike, properly cooked (and caught in less polluted waters than those in which I fished as a child), has a refined taste quite at variance with its troubling personal habits. This recipe, Pike with Butter Sauce, is one of the oldest and most traditional ways of cooking the "bandit of the Loire."

89

It's no surprise to learn that the pike is nicknamed *grand loup d'eau* (great water wolf). Its large mouth is filled with very sharp teeth, and many people cut off the head before cooking. Order it from your fishmonger, and ask for a river pike, rather than a pond one, because the flesh is white and cleaner. This is for a celebration meal.

Sole with Spinach   Serves 6

I love the simplicity of this recipe, *Sole aux Epinards*: the slight bitterness of the wilted greens contrasts with the melting sweetness of the sole and the creamy shallot sauce.

8 tablespoons (1 stick) unsalted butter
4 shallots, diced
Drizzle of olive oil
12 sole fillets
2 pounds spinach, trimmed and washed
⅓ cup heavy cream
Sea salt, to taste
Freshly ground black pepper, to taste
Lemon juice, to serve

Heat the broiler. Lightly oil the broiler rack and put it in the broiler for a few minutes to heat.

Meanwhile, heat 1 tablespoon of the butter in a medium saucepan, add the shallots, and cook gently for 10 minutes over low heat. Do not allow them to color.

Twist the sole fillets and place them on the rack—you should hear them sizzle as they touch it. Broil for 4 to 5 minutes, then remove them. Turn the broiler off.

Place the spinach in a large saucepan with 3 tablespoons of water and cook for about 3 minutes, stirring frequently. The spinach should soften and warm but retain its shape and texture. Put the spinach in a lightly buttered baking dish and arrange the sole fillets on top. Place in the turned-off broiler to keep warm.

Add the cream, salt, and pepper to the shallots and bring to a simmer. Cut the remaining 7 tablespoons of butter into small pieces and whisk a few pieces at a time into the simmering cream. When all the butter is added you should have a glossy sauce. Pour the sauce over the spinach and sole and finish with a squeeze of lemon.

Dover sole is superior to lemon sole. It has a firm but delicate texture and an exquisite taste, but with these qualities goes an expensive price tag. Lemon sole is more affordable, but you lose a little refinement in taste and texture.

Grilled Sole with Hollandaise
Serves 6

Sole is a delicious, tender fish that needs very little to enhance it (see page 93). *Sole à l'Hollandaise* is perfect—indeed, hollandaise sauce is a perfect accompaniment to all kinds of fish, as well as making asparagus or green beans into elegant vegetarian starters.

For the hollandaise
1½ cups (3 sticks) unsalted butter
2 tablespoons white wine vinegar
Juice of 1 lemon
6 large egg yolks

For the fish
12 sole fillets
Olive oil
Sea salt, to taste
Freshly ground black pepper, to taste
Bunch of flat-leaf parsley
3 lemons, halved

Make the sauce. Melt the butter slowly in a large saucepan. In a separate, small saucepan, heat the white wine vinegar and lemon juice until just boiling. Place the egg yolks in a 1-quart glass measuring cup or jar and blend with a hand-held blender, then slowly blend in the hot vinegar and lemon juice. Then, just as the butter comes to a boil, slowly pour it into the egg yolks and vinegar, constantly blending until all the butter is incorporated. Place the cup in a bowl of hot water and cover until ready to serve. If it is too thick, blend in a dash of hot water.

Heat the broiler and oil the broiler rack. Lay the sole fillets on the rack, drizzle with olive oil, season with salt and pepper, and broil for 5 minutes. Serve the sole with parsley sprigs, lemon halves, and the hollandaise sauce.

Simone's Marinated Tuna
Serves 6

Try this great dish, which should be made using only really fresh tuna, with steamed sliced new potatoes and a green salad. One of my great-aunt Simone's favorites, this dish is absurdly simple and quick to make.

Zest and juice of 6 lemons
⅔ cup olive oil
6 shallots, finely sliced
2 chiles, red or green, seeded and diced
Sea salt, to taste
Freshly ground black pepper, to taste
6 (5-ounce) tuna steaks

In a large, shallow or ceramic dish, mix the lemon zest and juice, olive oil, shallots, chiles, salt, and pepper. Finally, add the tuna fillets and refrigerate for 12 hours, occasionally turning the tuna in the marinade.

Heat a broiler or build a fire in an outdoor grill. Lightly oil the broiler or grill rack. Remove the tuna from the marinade. Broil or grill the tuna 1 to 2 minutes on each side for rare (4 minutes for well done). Serve at once, drizzled with the remaining marinade.

Mullet with a Mustard Crust Serves 6

Nothing could be easier than this recipe, *Rouget à la Moutarde*, but it is important that the fish is fresh from the sea to retain that perfect flavor. If mullet is unavailable, use other fish that weigh about one pound each, such as rainbow or brook trout or small red snapper. Serve with steamed potatoes and watercress.

6 red mullet, cleaned and scaled
⅔ cup grainy mustard, such as Meaux
2 tablespoons Dijon mustard
Olive oil

Heat the oven to 400°F.

Make three incisions across the fish on each side. Mix the mustards and spread thickly all over the fish, pushing some into each of the cuts. Lightly oil a large baking sheet, arrange the fish on it, and bake in the top third of the oven for 20 minutes. Serve at once.

When I was a child, red mullet were so common on Noirmoutier that you could almost catch them with your hands. It was our staple diet, grilled, barbecued, or as the principal ingredient for fish soup. Now these delicious fish are less easy to find, and are becoming quite a delicacy in expensive restaurants.

Poultry

Poultry has always been an important part of the French kitchen, which is hardly surprising in a country with such a strong farming and rural tradition. At one time, every country family kept hens, ducks, or geese, and these birds still tend to be associated with peasant dishes. Wild birds, too, have their place, especially in the more southern, mountainous regions of France, but many of these birds are difficult to find in North America, and we have adapted some dishes accordingly. Choose your poultry well. It is worth finding a good organic butcher or farmer who can advise and supply you.

In France, the age of the chicken usually determines the method of cooking. *Poussin* (3 months or less, average weight about 1 pound, serves 2): these birds should be split lengthways and grilled for 10 minutes on each side, or oven-roasted for 45 minutes to 1 hour. The flesh is extremely tender, with a very light taste. *Spring chicken* (3 to 6 months, average weight about 1¾ pounds, serves 4): roast in the oven for 20 minutes per pound. The flesh is tasty and tender. *Pullet* (7 to 8 months, average weight 4 to 6 pounds, serves 6): oven- or pot-roasted, the flesh is firm and of superior taste. *Hen* (12 months or more, average weight 3 to 6 pounds, serves 4): these birds are perfect for pot-roasting or braising. The taste is excellent, but unless cooked for a long time the flesh can be rather tough. Braise or stew for 3 to 4 hours. Ideal for country dishes such as *pot-au-feu* or *poule au pot*.

Duck flesh is dark and quite strong in taste. A duckling (2 to 3 months, average weight 1¾ pounds) can be pan-fried (10 to 12 minutes per pound) or roasted (15 minutes per pound). An older bird (4 months or more) is better roasted (18 minutes per pound) or braised (about 3 hours).

Goose is exceptional, but quite rich in fat. Don't be afraid of this; goose fat is wonderful for roasting potatoes and other vegetables. Roast the goose (age 6 to 8 months minimum, average weight 8 to 11 pounds) for 30 minutes per pound.

It's best to use young squab (3 to 5 months, average weight 10 ounces). The flesh is delicate and very slightly gamey, and can be roasted or sautéed (about 30 minutes, one bird serves 2).

These recipes are not designed with mass-produced poultry in mind. A fresh, well-fed, free-range chicken is a world away from a plastic-wrapped, watery chicken. Similarly, different birds have very different characteristics, determined by age, species, and diet, and you should bear this in mind when making your choice.

L'ARBRE à PAIN

Pain biologique   au leva

Mellionn

Madame Douazan's Poule au Pot   Serves 6

This centuries-old dish remains one of the simplest and most traditional methods of cooking chicken. Its patron is King Henri IV, who, concerned at the general poverty of his people, declared that under his reign even the poorest family should be able to have *poule au pot* every Sunday. Many people still use this sixteenth-century recipe, and this is Madame Douazan's version, which I first tried at her home, and which I always associate with her.

The people of Nérac in Gascony, where she lives, have a special affection for Henri IV. He had a castle there, with a wild park, La Garenne, where he spent many summers before coming to the throne. Local folklore has it that one year he fell in love with a girl, Fleurette, who drowned herself when the young Henri deserted her. La Garenne has a fountain with a marble statue in memory of her, and the Nérac *chocolaterie*, La Cigale, makes the most wonderful little bittersweet chocolates called *amours de fleurette*. They're a romantic lot in Nérac.

For the stuffing

8 ounces lean pork meat, minced
4 thick slices slab bacon, diced (see page 19)
4 ounces chicken livers, trimmed and roughly
    chopped
½ cup fresh bread crumbs, made from day-old loaf
4 shallots, diced
1 large egg, beaten
Bunch of flat-leaf parsley, chopped
2 garlic cloves, chopped
Sea salt, to taste
Freshly ground black pepper, to taste

1 (4- to 5-pound) chicken, preferably free-range
1¼ cups dry white wine
8 shallots, peeled
3 thyme sprigs
6 whole cloves
2 bay leaves
Sea salt, to taste
Freshly ground black pepper, to taste
12 small potatoes, peeled
4 carrots, cut into 2-inch lengths, or 12 baby carrots
1 turnip, cut into wedges, or 6 baby turnips
3 leeks, cut into 2-inch lengths, or 6 baby leeks
4 celery stalks, cut into 2-inch lengths
1 small green cabbage, cored and cut into wedges

First prepare the stuffing. Put the pork, bacon, and chicken livers in a large bowl. Add the bread crumbs, shallots, egg, parsley, garlic, salt, and pepper and mix everything well. You get a really good, even mix if you do this with your hands.

Heat the oven to 350°F.

Trim the chicken cavity of any excess fat and fill with the stuffing. Close up the neck and tail end of the chicken with a poultry needle and kitchen twine or by weaving bamboo skewers through the skin. Place the chicken in a large flameproof casserole and add 3½ cups water, the wine, shallots, thyme, cloves, bay leaves, salt, and pepper. Cover with a lid and bake for 1½ hours.

When the hour and a half has elapsed, add the potatoes, carrots, and turnip to the chicken in the pot, immerse them in the cooking juices, and cook the casserole for 15 minutes. Then remove the pot from the oven.

Carefully lift out the chicken and place it on a wire rack to drain off excess cooking juices. Return these juices to the pot and place the pot over moderate heat on the stove. Add the leeks, celery, and cabbage, cover with a lid, and cook at a rapid simmer for 10 minutes.

While the vegetables are simmering, remove and discard the skin from the chicken, and carve the meat and scoop out the stuffing.

Scoop the vegetables out of the cooking stock and serve them in individual, deep bowls with the chicken and the stuffing, and a generous ladle of the cooking stock.

Poule au pot is a peasant dish. It works best with an older bird, the lengthy cooking bringing out the stronger flavors. Cooked in this way, the meat becomes sweet and tender, but it is important to use a free-range chicken and good-quality vegetables. For maximum authenticity, serve the leftover cooking stock as a soup starter, with vermicelli.

Garlic Roast Chicken Serves 6

Garlic and rosemary give this dish, *Poulet à l'Ail*, a lovely Provençal flavor, filling your kitchen with the aromas of summer holidays all year round.

3 whole heads of garlic
1 (4- to 5-pound) chicken
4 rosemary sprigs
1 lemon, sliced
Sea salt, to taste
Freshly ground black pepper, to taste
Olive oil for the pan
2 tablespoons all-purpose flour
¾ cup dry white wine, plus more as needed
Bunch of flat-leaf parsley, finely chopped

Break the garlic cloves away from the bulbs, place in a small saucepan, cover with water, and simmer gently with a lid on for 30 minutes. Cool in the water. Drain the garlic cloves but don't throw the water away.

Heat the oven to 350°F. Carefully ease the skin of the chicken away from the breasts. Place a sprig of rosemary and a layer of lemon slices between the skin and the meat on each side. Stuff the cavity with the remaining rosemary and lemon slices, along with the garlic cloves. Season with salt and pepper.

Drizzle a roasting pan with olive oil, place the chicken in the pan, and roast according to weight: 20 minutes per pound, then 20 minutes extra. Transfer the chicken to a carving serving board and keep it warm while you make the sauce. Place the roasting pan over low heat on the stove, add the flour, and whisk well. Slowly pour in the reserved garlic water, whisking constantly. Add most of the white wine, bring to a boil, and adjust the consistency with extra wine if desired. Pass through a sieve into a saucepan, add the parsley, and bring to a simmer.

Carve the chicken and serve with the sauce.

Country Chicken Serves 6

This is a simple and tasty way of cooking young chickens, and it works very well with rice or pasta.

2 (3-pound chickens), cut into 6 pieces each
  (see Note)
12 ounces slab bacon, chopped (see page 19)
12 shallots, peeled
5 bay leaves
2 tablespoons olive oil
Sea salt, to taste
Freshly ground black pepper, to taste
3 tablespoons grainy mustard, such as Meaux
Bunch of French tarragon
1¼ cups dry white wine

Trim the chicken pieces of excess fat and place the chicken in a large bowl. Add the bacon, shallots, bay leaves, olive oil, salt, and pepper. Mix well, cover, and refrigerate to marinate overnight.

Heat the oven to 350°F.

Transfer the chicken and its marinade to a large roasting pan. Bake for 40 minutes.

Place the mustard in a small bowl. Strip the tarragon leaves from their stalks and finely chop the leaves. Add the leaves to the mustard along with the white wine, and mix well.

Remove the chicken from the oven and drain off the excess fat, then pour the mustard mixture over the chicken. Mix well and return to the oven to cook for 10 minutes.

Note: Ask your butcher to cut the chickens, or do it yourself with a large, sharp knife. For each chicken, you want two leg portions, two breasts, and two wings with some breast attached. First cut off each leg section (drumstick and thigh together) at the hip joint. Cut the chicken carcass lengthwise in half, cutting down one side of the backbone and the thin keel bone in the breast area. Cut off each wing, but include the top third of the breast on each portion.

Coq au vin: part of a dwindling tradition of old French dishes relying on wine, herbs, and a generous cooking time to ensure maximum tenderness and flavor.

Coq au Vin   Serves 6

This is another very old dish, invented—or so the story goes—by Julius Caesar. A group of Gauls had been cornered Asterix-fashion by one of Caesar's garrisons. To prove that they had plenty to eat, the Gauls sent out an old cockerel to the enemy, with a message around its neck saying "*Bon appétit!*" Caesar promptly invited the leaders of the Gaulish tribes to a dinner, in the course of which he served the cockerel (cooked to perfection in wine and rare herbs), promising the Gauls that if they surrendered, he would not only give them the recipe but also personally ensure that they and their descendants ate well and lived in prosperity forever. Did they believe him? The story doesn't tell . . . Make this dish the night before serving to let the flavors infuse and intensify.

1 (3½-pound) chicken, cut into 12 pieces (see Note)
2 cups red wine
5 ounces slab bacon, cubed (see page 19)
1 tablespoon olive oil
12 small shallots, peeled
8 ounces button mushrooms
1 garlic clove, chopped
3 tablespoons all-purpose flour
1½ cups chicken stock
2 thyme sprigs
2 bay leaves
Sea salt, to taste
Freshly ground black pepper, to taste
Bunch of flat-leaf parsley, chopped

Trim the chicken pieces of excess fat. For a really rich flavor, marinate the chicken pieces in the wine overnight. The next day, pour off the wine (keep it to cook the chicken) and dry the chicken well with paper towels to make sautéing easier.

Heat the oven to 350°F.

Put the bacon and oil in a large flameproof casserole and cook over medium heat for 3 minutes. Add the whole shallots and cook for 6 minutes until the shallots are browned, then add the mushrooms and garlic and cook for another 2 minutes, stirring well. Remove the ingredients from the pan and set them aside.

Place the chicken in the casserole and cook until golden and sealed all over—do this in batches to get a good even color. Remove from the casserole and set aside.

Reduce the heat, add the flour to the pan, and stir so it absorbs the fat. Don't forget to mix in all the colored cooking bits in the pan. Slowly stir in the reserved wine and the stock, and bring to a boil. Return the chicken, vegetables, and bacon to the casserole dish, along with the thyme, bay leaves, salt, and pepper. Cover and bake for 35 minutes. Just before serving, add the chopped parsley.

Note: Ask the butcher to cut up the chicken, or do it yourself with a sharp heavy knife. Cut the wings off of each chicken. Cut off each leg section, then cut at the joint to separate the drumstick and thigh. Cut the chicken in half lengthwise down one side of the backbone, then lengthwise through the thin keel bone at the breast area. Cut each breast portion crosswise into three somewhat equal portions. You will have two wings, two thighs, two drumsticks, and six breast portions.

Duck Confit Tart   Serves 6

Serve this tart warm, with a green salad alongside.

For the pastry

1⅓ cups self-rising flour

9 tablespoons (1 stick plus 1 tablespoon) chilled unsalted butter, cut into small pieces

3 tablespoons cold water, as needed

For the filling

1 (14-ounce) can duck or goose confit (see Note)

1 pound small boiling potatoes, peeled and boiled until tender

4 large eggs

⅓ cup milk

2 tablespoons heavy cream

Softened butter for the dish

4 shallots, diced

2 garlic cloves, chopped

Bunch of flat-leaf parsley, chopped

Sea salt, to taste

Freshly ground black pepper, to taste

To make the pastry, put the flour in a large bowl, add the butter, and rub together with your fingertips until the mixture resembles coarse bread crumbs. Using a round-bladed knife in a cutting motion, mix in the cold water to form a ball of dough, adding more water if needed. Turn out on a lightly floured surface and briefly knead until the dough is evenly mixed and smooth, then wrap in plastic and refrigerate to chill and rest for 30 minutes.

To make the filling, remove the meat from the can (refrigerate leftover fat for cooking potatoes or other recipes). Discard the skin and bones and roughly chop the meat. Slice the potatoes. In a bowl, beat the eggs with the milk and cream.

Heat the oven to 425°F.

Lightly butter a 9-inch pie plate. Roll out the pastry and use it to line the dish.

Add the confit, shallots, garlic, parsley, salt, and pepper to the pastry shell, then layer the potatoes over the top. Pour the egg mixture over. Bake in the center of the oven for 45 minutes. Reduce the oven temperature after 30 minutes if the tart is browning too much on top.

Note: Canned confit (poultry cooked and preserved in its own fat) can be purchased from many specialty food shops. Duck leg confit in vacuum-packed bags is available by mail order from D'artagnan (www.dartagnan).

This is one of those magical off-the-shelf dishes—that is, so long as you buy cans of *confit* when you are in France. The dish is straightforward to make and delicious to eat, and you can hunt down cans of *confit* in this country, too.

Crunchy Roast Duck Legs with Turnips   Serves 6

The meat content of a whole duck is low, which is why breasts (*magrets*) are so popular, while legs are an economical way to produce a delicious meal. Many different varieties of duck are cooked in France. The renowned breeds are Barbary, which are raised in the wild and have a gentle musky flavor; Nantes (or Challens, named after the marshland area where the duck lives), which have a delicately flavored flesh; and Rouen, the most well-known, which have an exceptionally fine flesh and a special flavor because they are killed in such a way (smothering) that the blood remains in the muscles.

1 tablespoon olive oil
6 duck legs (available at specialty butchers)
Sea salt, to taste
Freshly ground black pepper, to taste
6 shallots, peeled
12 baby turnips, trimmed
1 large tart apple, peeled, cored, and chopped
2 tablespoons all-purpose flour
1¼ cups hard apple cider
½ cup vegetable stock

Heat the oven to 400°F.

Place the oil in a large roasting pan and heat in the oven for 5 minutes. Stab the duck legs all over with a fork, rub with salt and pepper, then place in the hot pan and roast for 20 minutes. Turn the duck legs, and add the whole shallots and turnips to the pan. Baste with the fat, reduce the heat to 350°, and roast for another 20 minutes.

Turn the duck legs again, and add the apple, moving the roasting vegetables to ensure they cook evenly. Roast for 20 minutes or until the duck is golden and crunchy and the vegetables are soft and browned.

Remove the duck and vegetables from the pan and place them on a warm serving dish. Drain off excess fat (reserve it for roasting or sautéing potatoes) and add the flour to the pan, mixing it in vigorously to make a roux. Then slowly add the cider and vegetable stock, stirring well to mix in the roasting flavors in the pan. Cook on the stove over medium heat and bring to a simmer, constantly stirring. Check the seasoning, pour over the duck and the roasted vegetables, and serve.

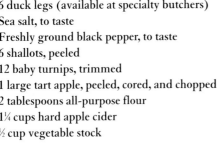

Duck Breasts in Orange
Serves 6

Magrets de Canard à l'Orange is a variation on the classic dish of duck with orange. Duck works well with sweet tastes, and this is a quick and stress-free version to prepare.

6 duck breasts with skin (*magrets*)
2 tablespoons unsalted butter
3 navel oranges
⅓ cup plus 1 tablespoon fresh orange juice
1 tablespoon red wine vinegar
1 tablespoon sugar
1 tablespoon cornstarch
2 tablespoons orange liqueur, preferably Grand
    Marnier
Sea salt, to taste
Freshly ground black pepper, to taste

Score the skin of each duck breast in a criss-cross pattern. Melt the butter in a large skillet and cook the duck breasts, skin side down, over medium heat for 10 minutes, until the skin is golden and the fat has run out of it.

Meanwhile, use a sharp knife to peel the oranges down to the flesh, cutting away all the white pith (do this over a plate to catch any escaping juice), and then cut into segments between the membranes. Remove any seeds.

Pour off the rendered fat in the skillet, then turn the breasts and cook flesh side down, still over medium heat, for 8 minutes. Remove the breasts from the pan and slice, arrange on warm plates, top with the orange segments, and keep warm.

Add the orange juice to the skillet (including any juice from the orange segments), along with the vinegar and sugar, and bring to a simmer. Mix the cornstarch with a little water to make a paste. Remove the skillet from the heat, and add the corn-starch paste. Return to the heat and stir well until the sauce is lightly thickened and smooth. Finally, add the Grand Marnier.

Pour the sauce over the sliced duck breasts, season with salt and pepper, and serve.

Fresh Foie Gras with Roasted Peaches   Serves 8

Foie gras has raised temperatures one way or another since Roman times. Horace's early writings describe a method of preparing geese that have been force-fed on figs. In the eleventh century, Sainte Radegonde—one of France's many culinary saints—had a dish of foie gras prepared for the soon-to be-canonized Bishop of Poitiers, who thanked her with poems and odes in her honor. The Marquis of Contades received a large fiefdom in Picardy from Louis XV as thanks for a gift of foie gras prepared by his pastry chef. Today it has become at the same time one of the most sought after and one of the most vilified foodstuffs in the world, appreciated by gourmets for its incomparable texture and taste, and denounced for the method of its production. It is, however, one of the oldest and most fabled ingredients of the French kitchen, and I'd hate to see political correctness send it into culinary extinction, the way of peacock hearts and larks' tongues in aspic.

1 fresh goose foie gras, about 1¾ pounds
Sea salt, to taste
Freshly ground black pepper, to taste
3 tablespoons Madeira
3 tablespoons cognac
1 cup plus 2 tablespoons (2¼ sticks) unsalted butter, plus more if needed
5 fresh peaches, pitted, each cut into 8 wedges
Grating of fresh nutmeg

Clean and trim the foie gras of any fibers or veins using a thin, sharp-bladed knife. Put it in a dish; add seasoning, Madeira, and cognac; then cover and marinate in the refrigerator overnight, turning it when you can in the evening before and the morning after.

The next day, remove the foie gras from the marinade and dry well with paper towels. Keep the marinade. Slice the foie gras crosswise on a slight diagonal into eight equal medallions.

Heat 6 tablespoons butter in a large skillet over high heat, and sear the foie gras on each side for 45 seconds—or more if you must. Remove the foie gras from the skillet and keep warm. Add more butter if needed and cook the peaches for 2 minutes, still over high heat. Arrange the peaches on warmed plates and set aside.

Pour the marinade into the skillet, bring to a simmer, then reduce the heat to low. Cut the remaining 12 tablespoons butter into small pieces and add to the skillet a few pieces at a time, whisking vigorously, to make a glossy sauce. Add the nutmeg.

Arrange the foie gras on top of the peaches, spoon over the sauce, and serve at once.

I picked up this way of cooking fresh foie gras—Fresh Foie Gras with Roasted Peaches—in the Gers, at the home of Madame Consularo, who runs the Château Bellevue in Cazaubon, near Eauze, and does all the cooking herself. She prepared this dish especially for me, and I've never had better.

To flambé is simply to pour liquor over food and ignite it. The flaming dish creates a sensation, but more than just a show, flambéing wonderfully enhances flavor, too. The easiest way is to heat the liquor in a small saucepan, carefully ignite it, and then pour the flaming liquid over the dish.

Quail with Cherries   Serves 6

Cailles Flambées is a simple but spectacular dish for a festive meal. Sour cherries have a brief summer season, and are worth searching out at farmers' markets and specialty produce markets.

1½ pounds sour cherries, pitted
⅔ cup red wine
Pinch of ground cinnamon
6 quail, cleaned with bones intact
    (not semi-boneless quail)
Sea salt, to taste
Freshly ground black pepper, to taste
2 tablespoons unsalted butter
1 tablespoon cornstarch
3 tablespoons kirsch
3 tablespoons cognac

Take a generous third of the cherries, about ½ pound, and blend them in a blender or food processor to chop, then press the pulp through a wire sieve to extract the juice; discard the pulp. Put the juice, remaining cherries, red wine, and cinnamon in a small saucepan, bring to a boil, then simmer gently for 30 minutes.

Meanwhile, season the quail on the inside with salt and pepper. Melt the butter in a large skillet, add the quail, and cook for 20 minutes, until browned all over.

Add the cherry mixture to the quail, cover them, and simmer for 15 minutes, turning the quail halfway through cooking.

Remove the quail from the sauce and place on a warmed serving dish. Use a slotted spoon to remove the cherries from the skillet, and scatter them over the quail. Transfer a spoonful of the liquid to a small bowl and set aside.

Increase the heat under the remaining sauce to reduce by one-third. Mix the cornstarch with the cooled liquid to make a thin paste, remove the sauce from the heat, and quickly stir in the cornstarch paste until smooth and blended. Return the sauce to the heat, stirring constantly until it thickens.

Pour the sauce over the quail, then combine, heat, and ignite the kirsch and cognac to flambé the dish just before serving.

Squab is tender and only slightly gamey, and the
peas give it a succulent sweetness. Use young squab
for this delicious dish, or try Cornish hen for another
version of it.

Squab with Peas Serves 6

Ideally, you should use 4- to 5-month-old squab and freshly shelled small peas for this traditional recipe, *Pigeon aux petits pois*. For the bouquet garni, tie together a bundle of fresh herbs. I use sprigs of parsley, thyme, sage, and rosemary, plus two bay leaves and a 2-inch piece of leek.

4 tablespoons (½ stick) unsalted butter
4 thick slices slab bacon (see page 19), cut crosswise
    into short strips
8 shallots, finely diced
3 squab, cut in half lengthwise
1 quart chicken stock
⅓ cup dry white wine
1 bouquet garni
Sea salt, to taste
Freshly ground black pepper, to taste
2 cups freshly shelled peas, about 2 pounds unshelled
1 head tender lettuce, such as bibb or Boston, cored
    and finely sliced
2 teaspoons light brown sugar
5 scallions, white parts only, finely sliced
Bunch of mint, finely chopped

Melt the butter in a large saucepan, add the bacon and shallots, and cook until just golden, then remove from the pan with a slotted spoon. Add the squab and lightly brown all over. Add the stock, wine, bouquet garni, salt, and pepper, then return the bacon and shallots and bring to a simmer and cook covered for 15 minutes.

Add the peas, lettuce, and brown sugar, stir well and simmer for 15 minutes, turning the squab so that they cook evenly.

Add the scallions for the final 2 minutes of cooking. Serve garnished with fresh mint.

Christmas Turkey with Chestnuts   Serves 8 to 10

The traditional French Christmas meal takes place on Christmas Eve and lasts long into the night. It's more usual to make this dish with goose, but you can use turkey—*Dinde aux marrons*—as long as you ensure the meat doesn't dry out. For me, chestnuts have always evoked the spirit of the season, and in France they are often used as a main vegetable rather than simply a garnish. They have a sweetness that works very well with roasted meat, and, fortunately, using the canned ones is just as good as buying them fresh. As for the turkey, order it well ahead of time, as small turkeys are not easy to come by.

For the stuffing

1 pound bulk pork sausage
1 (15½-ounce) jar vacuum-packed peeled chestnuts,
** finely sliced**
4 shallots, finely diced
1 large egg, beaten
2 garlic cloves, chopped
Bunch of flat-leaf parsley, chopped
Bunch of sage, chopped
Sea salt, to taste
Freshly ground black pepper, to taste

For the turkey

1 small (8½-pound) turkey with giblets
Sea salt, to taste
Freshly ground black pepper, to taste
8 tablespoons (1 stick) unsalted butter, softened
6 celery stalks, halved
6 carrots
6 red onions, peeled
5 cups chicken or turkey stock
6 tablespoons dry white wine
1 (15½-ounce) jar vacuum-packed peeled chestnuts,
** left whole**
2 tablespoons all-purpose flour

Heat the oven to 350°F.

To make the stuffing, combine the sausage, sliced chestnuts, shallots, egg, garlic, parsley, sage, salt, and pepper in a bowl. Mix well—this is best done using your hands.

Remove the giblets from the turkey and set aside, then season the inside of the turkey with salt and pepper and place the stuffing in the cavity. Generously smear the outside of the turkey with 4 tablespoons butter.

Grease a deep roasting pan with 1 tablespoon of the remaining butter and add the giblets, celery, whole carrots, and onions. Pour 2 cups of the stock and 3 tablespoons wine into the pan, and place the turkey on top. Cover generously with aluminum foil and cook in the center of the oven for 1½ hours.

Remove the turkey from the oven and reduce the heat to 300°F. Add the whole chestnuts and the remaining 3 cups stock and 3 tablespoons wine. Smear the turkey again with the remaining 3 tablespoons butter, cover again with foil, and roast for another 1 to 1½ hours. For the final 10 minutes of cooking, remove the foil and return the heat to 350°F. to give the turkey a golden skin.

Remove from the oven, lift the turkey onto a carving platter, and leave to rest in a warm place for 10 to 15 minutes—this allows the meat to relax and become more tender.

Discard the giblets. Carefully lift out the vegetables and chestnuts from the roasting pan and keep warm in a serving bowl. Place the roasting pan over medium heat and sift in about 1 tablespoon flour. Whisk vigorously and bring to a boil to make lightly thickened gravy—adjust with more liquid (stock or water) or a little more flour to get the right consistency. Pass through a fine sieve, then check the seasoning. Serve the turkey with the chestnuts and vegetables and sauce.

Meat

Most French families now rely on simple grilled or roasted meats, with little accompaniment other than a sauce made from the meat's own juices. However, many traditional dishes rely on sauces and long cooking times for their success. The following dishes are old favorites that have been slightly adapted to make them easier to make, but that still convey some of the many textures, smells, and tastes of the traditional French kitchen.

The essential thing when buying meat is to ensure it is of excellent quality. I find that, as with poultry, free-range organic meat is greatly superior in taste to the packaged, mass-produced variety. Befriend a good organic butcher, who will be able to recommend cuts of meat to suit the recipe you are planning, and bear in mind that whatever your personal standpoint on eating meat (and be it on ethical, taste, or health grounds), it is always beneficial to know that what you are eating has been treated with respect before it reaches your table.

The French have a good tradition of local butchers who will advise and, if necessary, prepare your meat for you. Our local butcher used to come in a van and deliver the Sunday roast to us at my grandfather's house.

Boucherie

Veal Parcels in White Wine Sauce is one of my mother's recipes that I associate with leisurely Sunday lunches in France with my grandparents. You can buy *paupiettes* ready-made in France, but they are quite easy to make at home—as our recipe demonstrates—and well worth the effort.

Veal Parcels in White Wine Sauce   Serves 6

The secret of this dish is in the cooking time: the longer you cook it, the better it gets, and if you make it the night before, the flavors will marry and intensify overnight, making a richer and tastier sauce.

For the filling

2 tablespoons olive oil
4 ounces mushrooms, chopped
1 red onion, diced
2 ounces ground pork
2 garlic cloves, chopped
Small bunch of flat-leaf parsley, chopped
Small bunch of sage, chopped
Sea salt, to taste
Freshly ground black pepper, to taste
¼ cup fresh bread crumbs

For the veal

6 veal scaloppini
2 tablespoons unsalted butter
3 red onions, peeled and cut in half
2 tablespoons all-purpose flour
2 cups dry white wine
6 small carrots, peeled
1¼ pounds small red-skinned potatoes, peeled

Heat the oven to 350°F.

Make the filling for the veal parcels. Heat the olive oil in a skillet, and sauté the mushrooms and the diced onion for 5 minutes. Add the pork, garlic, parsley, sage, salt, and pepper, and mix well; cook for another 5 minutes. Remove from the heat, mix in the bread crumbs, and cool a little.

Lay out the scaloppini on the work surface and divide the filling among them. Fold in the ends and then roll up each escalope, tying with kitchen twine to make little parcels.

Heat the butter in a skillet pan and fry the veal parcels together with the halved red onions until the veal is golden. Transfer the veal and onions to an overproof casserole with a lid.

Add the flour to the skillet and stir well, gathering all the tasty bits into the mix. Then slowly add the white wine, stirring well, and bring to a boil. Pass the sauce through a sieve over the veal and onions.

Put the casserole in the oven and bake, uncovered, for 20 minutes. Add the carrots and potatoes, cover with a lid, and cook for 55 minutes. Serve hot.

Lentil and Toulouse Sausage Casserole   Serves 6

This casserole, *Lentilles-Saucisses à l'Ancienne*, is another old favorite: easy to make, completely stress-free, and very versatile. It's great with country bread and strong red wine if you want a hot meal in a hurry. Toulouse sausages are made with pure pork and a generous amount of garlic. They vary from shop to shop according to personal recipes, so keep trying until you find your perfect one, or, if you prefer, use any other favorite sausage.

2 tablespoons olive oil
2 onions, diced
3 celery stalks, chopped
2 garlic cloves, chopped
3 large tomatoes, peeled and chopped
2 teaspoons tomato paste
3 thyme sprigs, leaves chopped
1 bay leaf
11 ounces lentils, preferably green *lentilles du Puy*
¾ cup red wine
6 Toulouse or other favorite cooked sausages
    (1½ pounds)
Large bunch of flat-leaf parsley
Sea salt, to taste
Freshly ground black pepper, to taste

Heat the oven to 400°F.

Heat the olive oil in a flameproof casserole; add the onions, celery, and garlic, and sauté for 5 minutes. Add the tomatoes, tomato paste, thyme, and bay leaf. Mix and cook for 5 minutes. Remove from the heat, add the lentils and red wine, stir well, then pour in enough water to cover, about 2 cups. Place the sausages on top, cover, and bake for 30 minutes. Stir in the parsley and season with salt and pepper just before serving.

Smoked Ham Winter Pot   Serves 6

Potée Auvergnate is a traditional French country dish. Every region has its variants, depending on the available vegetables, but this one is southern in character, thickened with chunky white beans and potatoes, perfect with a bottle of characterful red wine and an open fire.

1 pound dried cannellini beans, rinsed and
　　sorted for debris
1 (3-pound) shank-end smoked ham
6 small red onions, peeled
2 garlic cloves, chopped
1 tablespoon Dijon mustard
1 thyme sprig
1 bay leaf
Freshly ground black pepper, to taste
6 carrots, cut into 2-inch lengths
1 pound small red-skinned potatoes, peeled but
　　left whole
3 leeks, white and pale green parts only, cut into
　　2-inch lengths
Sea salt, to taste
7 ounces green beans, trimmed
Large bunch of flat-leaf parsley, finely chopped

Soak the white beans overnight in water. The next day, drain and rinse them well.

Place the ham in a large flameproof casserole, cover with water, and bring to a simmer, then cook for 10 minutes. Drain and discard the water. Return the ham to the casserole along with the drained beans, onions, garlic, mustard, thyme, bay leaf, and pepper. Barely cover with water, then gently bring to a boil, skimming off any residue. Cover and simmer for 1½ hours.

Add the carrots, potatoes, and leeks to the casserole, cover, and simmer for 15 minutes.

Check the seasoning—you may not need to add salt. Add the green beans and parsley and cook for 5 minutes.

Lift out the ham, allow all the stock to run back into the casserole, and place the ham on a large carving board or plate. Slice the ham and serve it with the vegetables and cooking stock.

Pork with Black Currant Sauce   Serves 6

Porc au Cassis is easy to make, and the result is a wonderfully intense concentration of autumn flavors.

14 ounces fresh black currants (or substitute one 16-ounce jar black currants in syrup, available at specialty food stores)

2 tablespoons sugar

1 tablespoon olive oil

2 pork tenderloins (about 1¾ pounds), trimmed of excess fat

Sea salt, to taste

Freshly ground black pepper, to taste

4 tablespoons unsalted butter

2 large tart apples, such as Granny Smith, peeled, cored, and sliced

Pinch of ground cinnamon

1 teaspoon black currant jam

Wash the currants, remove any stems, and place the fruit in a small saucepan with the sugar and 3 tablespoons water. Cover and gently bring to a boil, then remove from the heat. When they have cooled a little, drain the currants, reserving the juice. Separately reserve the currant juice and the currants. (If using currants from the jar, drain and reserve the syrup.)

Heat the oil in a large skillet and cook the tenderloin fillets over medium heat until golden all over. Season with salt and pepper, then cover and cook for 15 minutes. When cooked, transfer to a carving board and set aside while making the sauce.

Meanwhile, heat 1 tablespoon of butter in a saucepan and gently cook the apples for 10 minutes or until golden. Add the ground cinnamon.

Put the currant juice (or syrup) and the jam in the skillet and bring to a boil. Reduce the heat to low. Cut the remaining 3 tablespoons of butter into pieces and whisk it into the simmering juice to make a glossy sauce. Add the reserved currants.

Slice the tenderloins and serve on a bed of sautéed apples, topped with the currant sauce.

The sharpness of the black currants cuts through the richness of the pork in this dish. It works well on its own, or with steamed potatoes, which do not interfere with the balance of the dish.

Pork with Lentils   Serves 6

This simple dish, *Porc aux Lentilles*, combines Puy lentils and mustard to make a rich, creamy sauce. Puy lentils are grown only in the Velay region of France, and are famous for their green marbled appearance and excellent flavor. Here they carry the delicious sauce that goes so well with pork.

2 pork tenderloins (about 1¼ pounds), trimmed of
    fat
About 30 sage leaves
2 garlic cloves, cut into about 30 slivers
About 30 small pieces of lemon zest
Sea salt, to taste
Freshly ground black pepper, to taste
1 tablespoon olive oil
8 slices slab bacon (see page 19)
1 quart chicken stock
8 ounces green lentils (*lentilles du Puy*)
⅓ cup dry white wine
⅓ cup heavy cream or crème fraîche
1 tablespoon Dijon mustard

Heat the oven to 350°F.

Make slits all over each pork tenderloin with a small sharp knife and insert the sage leaves, garlic slivers, and pieces of lemon zest, then rub with salt and pepper.

Oil a baking sheet with the olive oil. Wrap the bacon around the pork. Place the tenderloins on the sheet and cook for 35 minutes.

Put the chicken stock and lentils in a large saucepan and simmer gently for 30 minutes, until the stock is absorbed.

In another saucepan, combine the white wine, cream, and mustard, season with salt and pepper, and heat through gently.

Slice the pork and serve with the lentils and mustard sauce.

Pork Chops with Mustard Sauce   Serves 6

Côtelettes de Porc à la Moutarde: a quick and easy way to make simple pork chops special. Good with Gratin Dauphinois (page 160).

6 center-cut loin pork chops with bone
Sea salt, to taste
7 tablespoons (¾ stick plus 1 tablespoon) unsalted
    butter
3 onions, finely diced
⅓ cup plus 1 tablespoon dry white wine
2 tablespoons Dijon mustard
4 ounces cornichons, sliced

Sprinkle the chops with salt. Melt 2 tablespoons of the butter in a large skillet, add the chops, and cook for 12 minutes on each side, or until golden brown all over. Remove the pork chops from the skillet and cover with aluminum foil to keep them warm.

Add the onions to the skillet and cook over gentle heat—do not frizzle or brown them. Pour in the white wine, increase the heat, and reduce the wine by half.

Mix in the mustard, reduce the heat again, then whisk in the remaining 5 tablespoons of butter in small pieces to form a smooth, glossy sauce. Finally, stir in the cornichons and serve the sauce with the pork chops.

Roast Pork with Figs   Serves 6

Pork skin adds extra flavor and creates a deliciously crunchy coating for the roast. While pork loins with skin are available in Europe, it is more than likely that your pork loin will be skinless. Many butchers sell pork skin by itself. Score a 12-ounce to 1-pound piece of skin in a close crisscross pattern, then wrap around the loin and tie securely with kitchen twine. If pork skin is unavailable, simply score the fat on the pork loin well.

2 tablespoons olive oil
3 pounds boned and rolled loin of pork, fat scored
Sea salt, to taste
Freshly ground black pepper, to taste
20 ripe figs
¾ cup dry white wine
2 tablespoons flour
⅓ cup vegetable water, such as that used to boil
    carrots or potatoes, or vegetable stock or
    plain water

Heat the oven to 400°F.

Put the olive oil in a large, heavy roasting pan and heat it in the oven. Rub the pork with salt and pepper. Take the pan out of the oven, put in the pork, and roll it in the hot oil to cover it evenly. Return the pan to the oven and roast the pork for 40 minutes, then reduce the temperature to 350°F. and roast it another 40 minutes. At this point, return the oven to its original temperature of 400°F.; this will help to get that final crunch on the roasted skin (if using).

Prick the figs all over with a fork and place them around the roasting pork, then add half the white wine and ⅓ cup water. After 15 minutes, remove the pan from the oven and baste the figs with the cooking juices, then roast for another 10 minutes.

Remove from the oven. Transfer the pork to a warm carving board or plate and allow it to rest for 10 minutes in a warm place. Remove the figs and keep them warm.

Make a sauce with the cooking juices: sprinkle the flour into the roasting pan and stir it well to absorb the fat and juices. Over medium-low heat, gradually add the remaining white wine and ⅓ cup water to the paste, mixing well. Allow to simmer and thicken. Check the seasoning for salt and pepper, adjust the consistency if necessary with extra water, and pass through a sieve.

Carve the pork and serve it with the figs. Serve the sauce separately or poured over the figs.

If you travel to Mont Saint-Michel, you will see the lambs grazing on the very green marshland by the water's edge, or even nibbling on the seaweed growing on the rocks.

Lamb Chops Vert Pré Serves 6

The crisp, fresh watercress is an excellent accompaniment to tender lamb and new potatoes (fingerlings are terrific with this). Traditionally, the lambs are fed on the grass of reclaimed land by the sea, and have a delicate, slightly salty taste, hence the name: *Côtelettes d'Agneau Vert Pré*. A perfect dish for springtime.

1 pound small new potatoes, scrubbed but unpeeled
12 loin lamb chops
Sea salt, to taste
Freshly ground black pepper, to taste
½ cup (1 stick) unsalted butter, at room temperature
Bunch of curly parsley, finely chopped
Juice of ½ lemon
7 ounces watercress, trimmed

Simmer the new potatoes in lightly salted water for 20 minutes or until cooked.

Heat the broiler. Arrange the chops on an oiled broiler rack, season with salt and pepper, and broil 6 minutes each side for rare, 8 minutes for medium, and 10 minutes for well done.

Cut the butter into tablespoons and mix in a bowl with the parsley and lemon juice, seasoning with salt and pepper.

Arrange the potatoes and watercress on plates, top with the lamb chops and scoops of the butter, and serve.

Lamb Navarin Serves 6

This dish would originally have been made with mutton, which would have needed a longer cooking time, but this version, *Navarin d'Agneau*, uses lamb for a sweet and tender casserole.

4 pounds boneless leg or shoulder of lamb, cubed

3 tablespoons all-purpose flour

3 tablespoons olive oil

1 quart vegetable stock

2 (14½-ounce) cans chopped tomatoes in juice, or
    1 pound fresh tomatoes, peeled

6 shallots, peeled and left whole

2 garlic cloves, peeled

⅔ cup red wine

1 tablespoon tomato paste

½ teaspoon sweet paprika, preferably a smoked
    variety, such as Spanish *Pimentón de la Vera*

2 marjoram sprigs

2 bay leaves

Sea salt, to taste

Freshly ground black pepper, to taste

12 ounces small red-skinned potatoes, scrubbed
    but unpeeled

8 ounces baby carrots, peeled

8 ounces baby turnips, peeled

Trim the lamb of any fat. Place in a bowl with the flour and toss to coat the cubes of meat evenly. Heat the olive oil in a large casserole, add just enough meat to cover the bottom of the pan, and brown the meat all over. Remove and repeat with the next batch until all the meat is browned. Return all the meat to the pan, add the stock, and bring to a simmer, mixing well. Add the tomatoes, shallots, garlic, red wine, tomato paste, paprika, marjoram, bay leaves, salt, and pepper. Bring to a boil and simmer gently for 1 hour, stirring from time to time.

Add the whole potatoes, carrots, and turnips to the casserole, making sure they are covered in liquid. You may need to add a little more stock or water at this point. Cook for 20 minutes or until the vegetables are tender, then serve.

APÉRITIF

LILLET

S'il vous plaît...

FORMULE LUNCH

Lillet **Blanc, Rouge ... Le verre** ....

ENTREE ou DESSERT + PLAT + 1 Vene de vin

19€

(Au choix dans le Marché

Braised Lamb Shanks   Serves 6

This dish has to be cooked slowly and gently for maximum flavor and tenderness. Serve with mashed potatoes.

For the marinade
1½ cups red wine
10 shallots, peeled and left whole
4 garlic cloves, crushed
1 tablespoon dried juniper berries
Zest of 1 lemon
1 rosemary sprig
Sea salt, to taste
Freshly ground black pepper, to taste

For the lamb
6 lamb shanks
3 tablespoons olive oil
10 ripe plum tomatoes, peeled, or use canned
    tomatoes
½ cup all-purpose flour
½ cup red wine
Bunch of flat-leaf parsley, chopped

Prepare the marinade. Put the wine, shallots, garlic, juniper berries, lemon zest, and rosemary in a large, shallow glass or ceramic dish. Add salt and pepper, then put in the lamb shanks and turn them to coat them well. Cover and refrigerate to marinate overnight.

The next day, heat the oven to 350°F.

Oil a large roasting pan with the olive oil. Transfer the lamb shanks and marinade to the pan, cover, and cook for 1 hour. Remove from the oven, turn the shanks, and add the tomatoes. Cook for about 1 hour, until the meat is tender.

When ready to serve, remove the shanks from the pan and keep them warm while you make the sauce. Put the roasting pan over low heat, sprinkle in the flour, and blend it with all the cooking juices. Gradually whisk in the red wine, bring to a boil, then stir in the parsley. Pour over the lamb shanks and serve.

White Sausage with Truffled Pasta   Serves 6

In France, *boudin blanc* (white pudding) is often given to children, and it remains one of the great memory dishes of my childhood, simply grilled or fried and eaten with buttered pasta. This rather more grown-up version—*Boudin Blanc aux Tagliatelles Truffées*—uses white truffle, which gives it a sophisticated, earthy flavor.

6 white sausages, such as French-style *boudin blanc*
    or bratwurst
1½ pounds fresh tagliatelle or fettuccine
2 tablespoons truffle oil
Sea salt, to taste
Freshly ground black pepper, to taste
1 white truffle

Heat the broiler. Place the sausages on the oiled broiler rack and broil for 12 minutes or until golden brown, turning occasionally.

Meanwhile, bring a large pan of lightly salted water to a boil, add the pasta, and cook until al dente. Drain and shake the colander to remove every last drop of water.

Warm a large serving bowl. Pour 1 tablespoon of truffle oil and a little salt and pepper into the dish and tilt to coat the inside of the bowl. Add the pasta, drizzle over the remaining 1 tablespoon oil, and sprinkle with a little more salt and pepper. Toss well.

Slice the sausages. Finely slice the white truffle using a truffle slicer. Add both to the pasta and serve at once.

Black Sausage and Apples   Serves 6

A classic Breton combination, *Boudin aux Pommes* is terrific with buckwheat crepes (page 49) or sautéed potatoes, and a crisp green side salad. *Boudin noir*, French blood sausage, is very simply made from seasoned pig's blood and fat, with regional additions that can vary from cooked onions to grated raw onions or even apples, prunes, or chestnuts.

Olive oil for sautéing
6 blood sausages, such as French-style *boudin noir,*
    cut into 1-inch slices
3 thick slices slab bacon, chopped (see page 19)
2 tablespoons unsalted butter
5 tart green apples, such as Pippin or Granny Smith,
    peeled, cored, and cut into wedges
Pinch of freshly grated nutmeg
Sea salt, to taste
Freshly ground black pepper, to taste

Heat a drizzle of oil in a large skillet, add the sausages and bacon, and cook over medium-high heat for 2 minutes on each side. Then reduce the heat to low.

While the sausages and bacon are cooking, melt the butter in another skillet, add the apples and nutmeg, mix, and cook over high heat for about 4 minutes or until the apples color and barely soften.

Add the apples to the sausage and bacon, season with salt and pepper, and cook for 5 minutes over low heat, then serve.

White sausage—*boudin blanc*—is a little harder to find in the U.S. than in France (look for bratwurst), but it is worth pestering your butcher for. This white sausage is particularly associated with Christmas, and made from finely ground poultry, veal, pork, or rabbit, mixed with spices and cream.

Filet Mignon with Tarragon   Serves 6

This simple but effective way of preparing steak dates back to the seventeenth century. Use lots of fresh tarragon for a sharp and delicious contrast with the creamy sauce.

2 tablespoons unsalted butter
6 medium portobello mushrooms, stemmed
Olive oil for sautéing
4 shallots, diced
⅓ cup plus 1 tablespoon dry white wine
3 tablespoons heavy cream
1 tablespoon grainy mustard, such as Meaux
1 garlic clove, chopped
Bunch of tarragon, chopped
Sea salt, to taste
Freshly ground black pepper, to taste
6 (5- to 6-ounce) filets mignon

Melt the butter in a large skillet over medium heat and cook the mushrooms on both sides until golden. Reduce the heat and keep warm until needed.

Heat a little olive oil in a saucepan over medium heat and sauté the shallots until soft and golden. Add the wine and simmer for 3 minutes, then reduce the heat and add the cream, mustard, garlic, tarragon, salt, and pepper to gently warm through. Do not allow to boil.

Heat a drizzle of olive oil in a large skillet over high heat and sauté the steaks, 1½ minutes on each side for rare, 2½ minutes on each side for medium, and 3 minutes on each side for well done (if you must!).

Serve the steaks on the cooked mushrooms, topped with the sauce.

This dish must have been a blessing for
seventeenth-century chefs. It takes scarcely
any time to cook, but is sophisticated enough
to please the most exacting individual.

Boeuf en Daube   Serves 6

This is the most traditional of the inland Provençal dishes. According to the old story, it was invented by a farmer's wife, who, having put a piece of beef in the oven to cook, began gossiping with a friend. She lost track of time, and found the pot dry and the meat burned. In an attempt to save dinner, she added more water to the pot, but forgot it again and it burned a second time. Desperate to hide her mistake, the farmer's wife added herbs, wine, and vegetables, so that by the end of the day the resulting dish was so sweet and tender that all her neighbors wanted the recipe. The secret is in the cooking time. My great-grandmother used to cook it in an earthenware pot over very low heat for three days, but this version has been reduced to a more manageable three hours. Serve with boiled new potatoes or noodles tossed in a little butter.

1 (750-milliliter) bottle of white wine

2 bay leaves

Sea salt, to taste

Freshly ground black pepper, to taste

1 (3½ pound) beef rump roast

4 tablespoons olive oil

2 onions, sliced

2 garlic cloves, chopped

3 tablespoons all-purpose flour, plus more for dusting

1 (14½-ounce) can chopped tomatoes in juice

1 cup Mediterranean black olives, pitted

1 tablespoon salted capers, rinsed of salt, or use drained and rinsed bottled capers

Zest of 1 orange

8 ounces carrots, chopped into 2-inch pieces

5 ounces cremini mushrooms

Bunch of flat-leaf parsley, chopped

Combine the wine, bay leaves, salt, and pepper in a nonreactive large bowl; add the rump roast and cover. Refrigerate to marinate overnight, turning from time to time.

Remove the beef from the marinade and pat it dry with paper towels. Retain the marinade.

Heat 2 tablespoons of the olive oil in a flame-proof casserole over medium-low heat. Add the onions and garlic and sauté gently for 8 minutes. Sprinkle in the flour and mix well, then pour in the marinade a little at a time, stirring constantly. When all the liquid has been stirred in, add the tomatoes, olives, capers, and orange zest, and bring to a simmer.

Heat the oven to 275°F.

Heat the remaining 2 tablespoons of oil in a large skillet over high heat. Dust the beef with flour and add it to the hot oil. Brown all over to seal.

Transfer the beef to the casserole, ladle some of the cooking liquid from the casserole into the skillet, and stir to lift off the meaty bits in the skillet. Pour these into the casserole. Bring the casserole to a simmer, cover with a lid, place in the oven, and bake for 2 hours.

When the 2 hours are up, add the carrots and mushrooms and then bake for 1 hour more.

To serve, lift the beef out onto a carving plate and cut it into thickish slices. Stir the parsley into the sauce, check the seasoning for salt and pepper, and spoon it, with the vegetables, over the sliced beef.

Rabbit with Chestnut Puree
Serves 6

Rabbit has always been a staple in France, and although in England it has been out of favor for many years, it has finally begun to make a comeback. This recipe—*Lapin à la Purée de Marrons*—makes the most of the rich, dark flesh of the rabbit and the sweet flouriness of the chestnuts. This is a perfect dish for autumn.

1 rabbit, cut into 6 pieces (ask your butcher to cut up the rabbit)
Sea salt, to taste
Freshly ground black pepper, to taste
5 tablespoons (½ stick plus 1 tablespoon) unsalted butter
5 ounces slab bacon, finely chopped (see page 19)
1 cup unsweetened chestnut puree
1¼ cups chicken stock
¾ cup dry white wine
7 ounces watercress

Heat the oven to 350°F.

Season the rabbit pieces. Melt the butter in a large flameproof casserole, add the rabbit along with the bacon, and toss to coat with the butter. Cover and cook in the oven for 20 minutes, then turn the rabbit, return the lid, and cook for another 20 minutes.

Remove the rabbit and set it aside in a warm place. Add the chestnut puree, stock, and wine to the casserole, place it over medium heat, and bring it to a boil. Use a whisk to work the puree into the mix, making a rich sauce.

Serve the rabbit with the chestnut sauce on a bed of watercress.

Rabbit with Red Rice   Serves 6

A warming country dish, in which the red rice absorbs and enriches the flavors of wine and rabbit.

2 tablespoons olive oil
1 rabbit, cut into 6 pieces (ask your butcher)
1 red onion, diced
2 thyme sprigs
1 bay leaf
8 ounces red rice
1 whole garlic bulb, cut in half crossways and roasted (see page 40)
1 pound ripe plum tomatoes, peeled, quartered, and seeded
⅓ cup dry white wine
Sea salt, to taste
Freshly ground black pepper, to taste

Heat the oven to 300°F.

Heat the olive oil in a flameproof casserole over medium heat. Add the rabbit and brown all over—about 10 minutes—then remove. Add the onion, thyme sprigs, and bay leaf to the casserole and sauté for 2 minutes. Add the rice, stirring well to coat the grains in oil and juices, then return the rabbit. Ease the garlic flesh out of its skin and stir it into the casserole with the tomatoes, wine, salt, and pepper. Add enough water so that the rice is covered with liquid. Mix well, bring to a boil, and reduce the heat to very low. Put the lid on and cook for 30 minutes. Stir from time to time and check that the rice does not stick to the bottom of the pan: add a little more wine, or water if the rice threatens to stick. Serve at once.

Red rice, grown in the Camargue region of France, is nuttier in flavor than Arborio rice, but does not demand as much cooking time as brown rice. It gives a lovely rich color to this autumn dish.

Vegetables

Traditionally, French dishes were not served with vegetables unless these were an integral part of the dish (such as *Pigeon aux petits pois, Dinde aux marrons*). Vegetable dishes would be served as a separate course, although nowadays this is not as common as it once was. As a result, there are many traditional French vegetable-based dishes that can very easily be adapted as main courses for people who prefer not to eat meat or fish.

Living as I do with two strict vegetarians, I find that vegetable dishes play a much greater part in my life than they did in my mother's. It's very hard to be vegetarian in France—although the markets are filled with the most fabulous produce—because to most French people the ethos of vegetarianism is incomprehensible and foreign (my mother still looks at Anouchka with suspicion, and asks her if she is eating properly, although you've never seen such a healthy child).

I am quite happy to prepare and eat vegetarian food at home (although many nonvegetarian French dishes have too many personal and cultural associations for me ever to forsake them completely). However, as with all the recipes in this book, the quality of the ingredients is the secret to the success of the dish. Locally grown produce in season is by far the best, and you should try to make the most of it whenever possible. There is little to beat the taste of freshly picked green peas, or buttered new potatoes, or fresh, tender green beans, or sun-warmed tomatoes drizzled with lemon juice and oil.

And as in so many things to do with food, the anticipation—waiting for the strawberries or the young sprouting broccoli to come into season; enjoying the autumn flavors of pumpkin or blackberries or squash—becomes a significant part of the pleasure.

French markets are one of the great pleasures of
the summer. Stalls of brightly colored fruit and
vegetables, spices, olives, and mushrooms are as
much a delight to the eyes as to the palate, and in
the warmth of the morning sun, the scent is heavenly.

LE ROUGE GO...

ts Artisa

s d'Epices, Co

Anouchka's Pumpkin Seed Mushrooms   Serves 6

My daughter invented this recipe when she was three years old by accidentally dropping the contents of a box of pumpkin seeds into a dish I was preparing. The child shows promise. . . . Serve with baked potatoes or pasta, or on toast with a green salad.

12 ounces cremini mushrooms
Olive oil
2 tablespoons unsalted butter
4 shallots, chopped
3 tablespoons shelled pumpkin seeds
3 garlic cloves, crushed, peeled, and chopped
⅔ cup dry white wine
Juice of ½ lemon
Sea salt, to taste
Freshly ground black pepper, to taste
2 teaspoons grainy mustard, such as Meaux
3 tablespoons heavy cream

Separate the stems and caps of the mushrooms. Finely chop the stems and slice the tops.

Heat a little olive oil with the butter in large skillet and cook the mushroom stems and caps over medium heat, stirring constantly, until they are golden brown, about 8 minutes. Add the shallots, pumpkin seeds, and garlic and cook for a further 4 minutes. Add the wine, lemon juice, salt, and pepper, simmer for 4 minutes, then stir in the mustard and cream. Stir well, simmer for 2 minutes, and then serve.

Imbach Mushrooms   Serves 6

When I was small we sometimes went hunting for mushrooms in the woods with our friends the Imbachs. I don't remember actually finding any myself (except for once, when I found a puffball the size of a beach ball, and was very disappointed to be told we couldn't eat it), but that didn't stop me from trying. This dish is great with any kind of mushrooms, although the larger ones do tend to have more flavor.

12 medium portobello mushrooms, stems removed
1 cup red wine
⅓ cup plus 1 tablespoon olive oil
⅓ cup cognac
3 garlic cloves, chopped
Sea salt, to taste
Freshly ground black pepper, to taste
Large bunch of flat-leaf parsley, finely chopped
6 baguette slices

Place the mushrooms, wine, olive oil, cognac, garlic, salt, and pepper in a large bowl and toss well to coat the mushrooms. Marinate at room temperature for 1 hour.

Heat the oven to 350°F.

Put the mushrooms with their marinade on a rimmed baking sheet and bake for 6 minutes, then turn them over and bake for 4 minutes. Move the mushrooms around to ensure even cooking.

Sprinkle the parsley over the mushrooms and return to the oven for 2 minutes.

Lightly toast the slices of baguette. Pile the mushrooms on the warm bread and drizzle with any cooking juices.

This dish is perfect to make with autumn field mushrooms, and tastes so good that I can quite happily eat it as a main course with a green salad. Porcini mushrooms—*Boletus edulis*—also work very well prepared in this way, if you are lucky enough to find some, or you could try a mixture of wild and cultivated mushrooms.

Although this is, strictly speaking, an Italian dish,
I couldn't resist including it here as it is one of the great
comfort foods of winter. I like to make it with the local
Noirmoutier potatoes, an ancient variety dating back to
the sixteenth century, and perfect for this dish.

Spinach Gnocchi Serves 6

This is a great cold-weather dish: rich, warm, and flavorsome. Ideal for lazy nights in.

1½ pounds baking potatoes, peeled and cut into pieces
12 ounces spinach, trimmed and washed
1 cup all-purpose flour, plus extra for dusting
1 egg yolk
Sea salt, to taste
Freshly ground black pepper, to taste
5 tablespoons butter, plus more for the dish
4 ounces blue cheese, such as Roquefort
Bunch of basil

Place the potatoes in a saucepan of lightly salted boiling water and simmer for 20 minutes. Drain, return to the pan over low heat, and shaking the pan, allow the excess moisture to evaporate. Mash the potatoes until smooth.

Cook the spinach in a large saucepan over medium heat with no added moisture, mixing constantly until wilted and soft. When cooked, place in a clean kitchen towel. Gather the corners together and twist tightly to squeeze out every last drop of moisture, then finely chop the spinach.

Place the mashed potatoes, spinach, flour, egg yolk, salt, and pepper in a large bowl and mix until evenly blended and a soft pliable dough forms. Dust your hands and a board or tray with flour. Take small nuggets of the dough, roll into balls, and place them on the board. You should end up with about 60. Using a fork, gently flatten each ball, allowing the tines of the fork to make indentations across the top.

Heat a large pan of lightly salted water to a boil, then reduce the heat. To the simmering water add just enough gnocchi so that they have room to roam around, and cook for 2 minutes, or until they rise to the surface. Remove and drain well, and cook the next batch.

Heat the oven to 350°F. Lightly butter a large low-sided baking dish.

Place a layer of the cooked gnocchi in the dish, then crumble in some of the blue cheese. Continue to layer the gnocchi and cheese, adding salt and pepper and the butter cut up into little pieces as you go. Cook until golden and bubbling, about 10 minutes. Tear up the basil, scatter it over the top, and serve.

Gratin Dauphinois   Serves 6

The ultimate potato dish. It's so good that I'm quite happy to have this as a main course, although it also works very well as an accompaniment to meat, fish, or green vegetables.

2¼ pounds baking potatoes
1 garlic clove, crushed
5 tablespoons (½ stick plus 1 tablespoon) unsalted
    butter, plus softened butter for the dish
2½ cups half-and-half
Sea salt, to taste
Freshly ground black pepper, to taste
1 cup (4 ounces) shredded Gruyère

Heat the oven to 300°F.

Peel the potatoes and slice them thin using a mandoline or a food processor. Place the potato slices in a large bowl of cold water and move them around to get rid of excess starch. Drain well and dry thoroughly; use a salad spinner or else put the slices in a kitchen towel, gather the corners together, go outside, and swing your arm as fast and vigorously as you can.

Rub a large shallow baking dish with the garlic clove and a little butter.

Put the butter with the cream in a large saucepan and bring just to a boil. Finely dice what's left of the garlic and add it to the butter and cream, along with the sliced potatoes, salt, and pepper. Gently simmer for 8 minutes.

Transfer to the prepared dish, spread evenly, and top with the Gruyère and a little more salt and pepper. Bake for 1½ hours. Serve hot.

Gratin Dauphinois has everything you need in a main course: a creamy, satisfying texture, lots of flavor, and a golden, crispy surface. The story I heard was that it was created for the *dauphin*—the young prince soon to become Henri II—to encourage him to eat his vegetables.

Gratin Dauphinois is well worth the preparation it takes. Slice the potatoes on a mandoline (you can buy these very reasonably), then rinse the slices in fresh water to get rid of starch. Dry them in a salad spinner or a kitchen towel. The rest is easy, but do not rush the cooking. The result is perfection.

Boulangère Potatoes   Serves 6

This dish takes time—don't rush it! The result is worth it: meltingly tender potato slivers topped with a crunchy, golden crust like French bread, hence the name Pommes Boulangère.

2¼ pounds baking potatoes
2 onions
2 tablespoons unsalted butter, plus softened butter
    for the dish
Few thyme sprigs
Sea salt, to taste
Freshly ground black pepper, to taste
1¼ cups chicken or vegetable stock, heated

Heat the oven to 350°F.

Peel the potatoes and slice them very thin using a mandoline or a food processor. Slice the onions in the same way.

Butter a shallow baking dish and make layers of the potatoes and onions, with the thyme leaves (stripped from the stalks), salt, and pepper sprinkled over each layer. Finish with a layer of potatoes and try to make a neat overlapping pattern with them. Using the flat of your hand, press down the potatoes firmly.

Pour in the hot stock. Cut the butter into little pieces and dot the top with them. Cover with aluminum foil and bake for 1 hour.

Remove the foil and bake for 30 minutes. The potatoes should be soft all the way through and the top layer golden brown.

Mashed Potatoes with Nutmeg   Serves 6

Properly mashed potatoes are one of life's small but significant delights. Having tasted this, I just can't understand the instant stuff at all.

3 pounds baking potatoes
1¼ cups milk
¾ cup (1½ sticks) unsalted butter
1 large egg
¼ teaspoon freshly grated nutmeg
Sea salt, to taste
Freshly ground black pepper, to taste

Peel the potatoes, cut into pieces, place in a saucepan of lightly salted boiling water, and simmer for 20 minutes. Drain well, return to the pan to low heat, and shaking the pan, allow the excess moisture to evaporate. Mash the potatoes until smooth—for perfect mashed potatoes, try using a hand-held ricer.

Place the milk and butter in a small saucepan over medium heat and gently bring to a boil. Slowly pour the hot milk into the potatoes, mixing well with a rubber spatula. Break in the egg and beat. Finally, add the nutmeg, salt, and pepper. Mix well, taste, and adjust to your personal choice. Serve at once.

Sautéed Potatoes   Serves 6

Pommes de Terre Sautées are an excellent accompaniment to roast meat or fish, although I think they are good enough to eat as a main course with a crunchy green salad.

4 pounds baking potatoes
½ cup olive oil
Sea salt, to taste
Freshly ground black pepper, to taste

Peel the potatoes and parboil whole in lightly salted, gently boiling water for 12 minutes. Drain and slice into ¼-inch-thick rounds. Heat the oven to 350°F.

Divide the oil between two large skillets and heat. Place a layer of potatoes over the base of each pan and cook for 5 minutes on each side until golden.

Remove the potatoes with a slotted spoon and place in a roasting pan with a crumpled up piece of parchment paper on the bottom (this prevents the potatoes on the bottom from going soggy). Keep warm in the hot oven. Repeat until all the potatoes are cooked.

Sprinkle with salt and pepper, and serve at once.

Roasted Asparagus Spears   Serves 6

This is a simple and delicious way to prepare asparagus, and it works wonderfully in salads.

1 pound asparagus spears
3 tablespoons olive oil
Juice of 1 lemon
Dash of balsamic vinegar
Sea salt, to taste
Freshly ground black pepper, to taste
At least 4-ounce piece of Parmesan (you may
    not use all of the cheese)

Trim the white ends from the asparagus; I sometimes like to cut at an angle.

Heat the oven to 400°F.

Drizzle a large nonstick baking sheet with the olive oil, add the asparagus, toss them in the oil, then roast for 10 minutes. The asparagus around the edge of the tray may be better roasted, so cook the middle pieces for a few minutes longer if needed.

Transfer the roasted asparagus to a serving dish and add the lemon juice and balsamic vinegar. Season with salt and pepper. With a vegetable peeler, carve ribbons of Parmesan over the top. Serve hot or at room temperature.

Snap up fresh green asparagus in season and prepare
this wonderful—and wonderfully easy—dish. Either eat
the asparagus soon after roasting, while still hot, or save
to eat at room temperature later in the day—on a picnic,
perhaps.

Green Beans with Pine Nuts
Serves 6

At my grandparents' house I remember throwing closed pinecones into the open fire to make the pine nuts pop out ready-toasted—this has the advantage of being alarming to adults and potentially hazardous, and is therefore tremendous fun. Nowadays you can buy pine nuts at the supermarket, which is less fun but much easier. These green beans are great served with roast lamb, or added to lightly cooked pasta with chopped tomato and a squeeze of lemon.

14 ounces *haricots verts* or thin green beans, trimmed
¼ cup pine nuts
3 tablespoons dry white wine
2 tablespoons unsalted butter
Sea salt, to taste
Freshly ground black pepper, to taste

Plunge the beans into lightly salted boiling water and cook for 2 minutes.

Heat an empty nonstick skillet, and sauté the pine nuts without any additional oil—vigilantly—until the nuts turn golden brown. Take care: nothing seems to happen, then suddenly the pine nuts color.

Drain the beans well and place in a large saucepan with the wine and butter. Cover and cook for 1 minute, add the toasted pine nuts, toss, season with salt and pepper, and serve.

Zucchini with Lemon Butter
Serves 6

My grandfather used to grow giant (and quite inedible) summer squash in his garden, living by the rule that the bigger they got, the better they were. These zucchini, however, are at their most sweet and tender when small, and make an excellent accompaniment to fish or vegetable dishes.

3 tablespoons unsalted butter
2 tablespoons olive oil
6 medium zucchini
Zest and juice of 1 lemon
Sea salt, to taste
Freshly ground black pepper, to taste

Place the butter and oil in a large skillet and gently heat. Cut the zucchini at an angle into slices about 1 inch thick. Increase the heat under the skillet and add a layer of the zucchini, frying them on each side until golden. Remove and keep warm, and repeat until all the zucchini are cooked. Return the zucchini to the pan, add the lemon zest and juice, salt, and pepper; toss and serve at once.

Ratatouille can be as simple or as complicated as
you want to make it. The main rule is that the
longer you cook it, the better it becomes. So, as
with all casseroles, make it a day in advance to
allow the flavors to merge.

Ratatouille Serves 6

For variations, try using red wine instead of water, or chiles for extra bite. This is very good with Anouchka's Chile Garlic Bread (page 61).

9 tablespoons olive oil
2 red onions, chopped
2 garlic cloves, chopped
3 red bell peppers, seeded and cut into chunks
2 eggplants, cut into chunks
4 zucchini, cut into chunks
3 (14½-ounce) cans chopped tomatoes in juice, or
    2 pounds ripe fresh tomatoes, peeled
Bunch of oregano, chopped
Bunch of marjoram, chopped
Bunch of flat-leaf parsley, chopped
Sea salt, to taste
Freshly ground black pepper, to taste

Heat 3 tablespoons of the olive oil in a large saucepan over medium heat, add the onions and garlic, and sauté for 3 minutes. Add the peppers, eggplants, and zucchini; mix well and cook for 5 minutes or until the vegetables have gained a little color. Then add the tomatoes, 1⅔ cups water, the oregano, marjoram, parsley, salt, and pepper; mix well and simmer gently over medium-low heat for 1 hour, stirring from time to time. Stir in the remaining 6 tablespoons olive oil and check the seasoning. Serve hot or at room temperature.

Spiced Red Cabbage   Serves 6

This wonderfully comforting dish for autumn and winter is filled with rich, sweet flavors. Best made a day ahead and reheated, it works very well with baked ham, duck, or even roast chicken, although I am happy to eat it on its own.

3 tablespoons unsalted butter
1 tablespoon olive oil
1 small red cabbage, cored and finely sliced
1 red onion, finely sliced
1 hot red chile, seeded and finely sliced
    (seeds included if you like the heat)
⅓ cup plus 1 tablespoon red wine vinegar, or
    3 tablespoons balsamic vinegar
⅓ cup light brown sugar
½ teaspoon ground allspice
½ teaspoon ground cloves
Sea salt, to taste
Freshly ground black pepper, to taste

Melt the butter with the oil in a saucepan over medium heat; add the red cabbage, onion, and chile, stir well, and cook for 10 minutes. Add the vinegar, brown sugar, allspice, cloves, salt, and pepper, then ¾ cup water; mix well and bring to a boil. Reduce the heat to low, cover, and simmer the dish for 1 hour, checking frequently. If the mixture becomes dry during cooking, add a little more water. Serve hot or reheated.

Roasted Vegetables with Couscous   Serves 6

I'm a great fan of couscous, which I use with all kinds of ingredients as an alternative to rice or pasta. It's ridiculously quick and easy to make, healthy, delicious, and has the capacity to soak up flavors, making it extremely versatile. This is a vegetarian version, which can be enjoyed entirely on its own, or as an accompaniment to a meat or fish dish, or with a salad. Try it with a handful of raisins and chopped apricots, and plenty of chopped fresh mint.

4 tablespoons olive oil, plus a little extra for serving
2 onions, peeled and cut into wedges
3 carrots, cut into chunks
2 parsnips, cut into chunks
2 shallots, peeled
3 garlic cloves, chopped
1 hot red chile, seeded and finely sliced
    (seeds included if you like the heat)
1 teaspoon sweet paprika
½ teaspoon ground cinnamon
½ teaspoon coriander seeds, crushed
½ teaspoon cumin seeds, crushed
4 cardamom pods, crushed
1 pound ripe plum tomatoes, peeled
2 zucchini, thickly sliced
Large pinch of saffron
Sea salt, to taste
Freshly ground black pepper, to taste
14 ounces couscous
5 tablespoons (½ stick plus 1 tablespoon) unsalted
    butter
Bunch of flat-leaf parsley, chopped
Bunch of cilantro, chopped
Dash of balsamic vinegar

Heat the oven to 375°F.
Heat the olive oil in a large, heavy-bottomed roasting pan directly over medium heat. Add the onions, carrots, parsnips, and shallots and cook for about 10 minutes or until golden, stirring frequently. Add the garlic, chile, paprika, cinnamon, coriander, cumin, and cardamom and stir well,

coating the vegetables with all the spices. Cook for a further 4 minutes, then remove from the heat and stir in the tomatoes, zucchini, saffron, salt, and pepper. Transfer to the oven to roast for 40 minutes. Check after 30 minutes, adding a little water or vegetable stock if needed.

Place the couscous in a large bowl and cover with boiling water to a level of 1 inch above the grains. Mix well and leave to stand for 5 minutes. Meanwhile, melt the butter in a small saucepan, add the chopped parsley and cilantro, and cook for 1 minute. Pour over the couscous, mix well, and season it.

Take the vegetables out of the oven, drizzle with olive oil and balsamic vinegar, and serve them on top of the couscous.

My daughter loves making these crisp roasted peppers
and designing new fillings for them. Try them with rice,
or couscous with dried fruit, or slices of pancetta—the
variations are endless.

Baked Red Peppers Serves 6

Use good, well-ripened red peppers for a cheery, colorful summer dish.

3 red bell peppers
Olive oil
1 large red onion, peeled and cut into wedges
1 medium fennel bulb, trimmed and cut into wedges
3 garlic cloves, sliced
Sea salt, to taste
Freshly ground black pepper, to taste
7 ounces goat cheese

Heat the oven to 250°F.

Cut the peppers in half lengthwise and remove and discard the entire core. Lightly oil a baking sheet and place the peppers on it.

Put the onion, fennel, and garlic in a bowl, drizzle over some olive oil, and add salt and pepper. Mix to coat the vegetables in oil and seasoning, and then divide them among the peppers, stuffing them inside the pepper halves. Bake for 1 hour and 20 minutes.

Remove the stuffed peppers from the oven and increase the heat to 375°F. Slice the goat cheese and arrange it over the peppers. Return the baking sheet to the oven and roast for 5 minutes, until the cheese is bubbling. Serve hot.

Desserts

The names of French desserts are a translator's nightmare: *le gâteau* is a generic term for "cake," although perplexingly, *le cake* refers to a kind of tea bread. The word *tarte* covers a wide variety of recipes, from the open fruit tarts to the upside-down *tarte tatin*, but there is no true word for "pie"—unless we count *tourte,* which is most often used as a term of abuse. And as for translating some of the bizarre names of the confections to be found in French pâtisseries—it is almost impossible. Many of them are religious in origin—Saint-Honoré has a cake named after him, filled with whipped cream and sugar.

But the French have a longstanding tradition of irreverence toward the Catholic Church that extends even into the kitchen. How else can we explain the *religieuse*—that little cake made up of two choux buns one on top of the other, so that it looks like a fat little nun? Or even the deliciously named *pet de nonne?* These small, chocolate-coated pastries are now served under a respectable alias in some of our more elegant restaurants, but the original name—still gleefully used in many regions of France—translates as "the nun's fart." Remember that, next time you eat a *profiterole*.

It is a peculiar fact that the French, who make
the most wonderful cakes, rarely eat dessert on a day-to-
day basis. Fruit, yogurt, and cheese are the most usual
endings to a meal, but on Sundays and during special
celebrations, desserts really come into their own.

Blueberry Tart   Serves 6

Blueberries are plump berries that develop great taste when cooked. Bilberries are tiny and grow wild in Europe, and have a sharp, tart flavor. The two are sometimes confused because of the similarity of the names. I like to make this tart with bilberries—*Tarte aux myrtilles*—which are hard to find but worth it (this is the only thing that motivates me to brave the moors and pick a batch once in a while), but you can use any small berry in season; and besides blueberries, which the tart shown here is made with, blackberries, raspberries, and black currants all work well. The *pâte brisée* is crumbly and light, like freshly baked shortbread, and although it is very easy to prepare, this is the kind of dessert that always gives me a sense of achievement.

For the pâte brisée
1¾ cups all-purpose flour
12 tablespoons (1½ sticks) chilled unsalted butter, cut into small pieces, plus extra for the tart pan
1 tablespoon sugar
1 large egg
½ tablespoon cold water

For the filling
1 pound blueberries or other berries, stems removed
¾ cup heavy cream
⅔ cup sugar, plus more for sprinkling
2 large eggs
3 tablespoons all-purpose flour
1 tablespoon crème de cassis

Make the crust. Rub the flour and butter together with your fingertips until the mixture looks like coarse bread crumbs. It really helps to work in a cool kitchen and have cool fingers. Mix in the sugar, then add the egg and water, using a round-ended knife in a cutting motion to combine the ingredients until they form a dough ball. Put the ball on a cool, floured work surface and briefly knead with the palm of your hand to ensure an evenly blended dough. Wrap and refrigerate to chill and rest for 40 minutes.

Lightly butter a 10-inch tart pan with a removable bottom. Lightly flour a cool surface and roll out the chilled dough slightly wider than the pan (because you do not want to have to stretch it). As this is a high-butter-content pastry, take care not to let the pastry stick to the surface—keep dusting lightly with flour. Line the pan with the dough, letting the excess dough hang over the edges. To trim it, simply roll the pin over the tart pan. Refrigerate the lined tart pan for 20 minutes.

Heat the oven to 400°F.

Place the berries in the lined pan. In a medium bowl, mix the cream, sugar, eggs, flour, and liqueur until smooth and pour over the fruit. Lightly sprinkle with a little extra sugar and bake for 35 minutes. Serve cooled, if you can wait.

You find fruit tarts like this one in all the most elegant *pâtisseries* in France; my mother used to buy them for birthdays and saints' days, but they are far too good to be kept for special occasions.

Strawberry Tart   Serves 6

This spectacular tart, *Tarte aux Fraises*, can also be made with any other fresh fruit—try raspberries, plums, peaches, or apricots—and it looks terrific every time. These desserts were what I always had on festival days as a child, and their jewel colors and wonderful textures and scents will give an instant carnival atmosphere to any table. The tarts don't keep well, so eat on the same day: though who could not? Serve with thick cream.

For the almond pastry
1⅓ cups all-purpose flour
½ cup (2 ounces) ground almonds (use a rotary
    grater or food processor)
¾ cup plus 2 tablespoons (1¼ sticks) chilled unsalted
    butter, cut into small pieces, plus
    softened butter for the pan
⅔ cup packed light brown sugar
2 to 3 large egg yolks, beaten

For the filling
½ cup red currant jelly
2 pounds strawberries, tops trimmed

Make the pastry. Mix the flour and ground almonds. Rub the butter into the flour with your fingertips until it resembles coarse bread crumbs. (Remember: cool kitchen and cool fingers, if you can.) Mix in the brown sugar. Using a round-ended knife in a cutting motion, add enough of the egg yolks until the ingredients come together into a dough ball. Lightly knead the dough on a cool, floured work surface to ensure an evenly blended pastry. Wrap and refrigerate to chill and rest for 40 minutes.

Lightly butter a 10-inch tart pan with a removable bottom. Roll out the pastry on a lightly floured surface, then line the pan. Refrigerate to chill and relax for 20 minutes.

Heat the oven to 375°F.

Line the pastry shell with parchment paper and dried beans or pastry weights and bake for 20 minutes. Then remove the paper and beans, reduce the heat to 300°F., and bake for 25 minutes, until the tart shell is golden and set. Remove from the oven and cool.

Gently heat the jelly in a small saucepan over low heat until thin and smooth. Allow the jelly to cool a little.

Carefully release the cooled tart shell and transfer it to a large, flat plate. Do take care, as this pastry is fragile. Cut any large strawberries into smaller pieces, then pile the fruit into the case. Spoon the warm jelly over the strawberries to give an even coating, leave to set for 1 hour, then serve.

Lemon Tart   Serves 6

This is my great-aunt Simone's version of an old and well-loved dish, *Tarte au Citron*. The creamy filling has an intense, sunny flavor; I like it best in winter, when I eat it to counteract seasonal blues. It's one of Anouchka's favorite desserts, too, and it's easy enough to make that she can help me. I have to watch her carefully, though—she eats the lemons when I'm not looking!

For the **pâte brisée**
2 cups all-purpose flour
12 tablespoons (1½ sticks) chilled unsalted butter, cut
  into small pieces, plus softened butter for the pan
1 tablespoon sugar, preferably superfine sugar
1 large egg beaten with 2 teaspoons water

For the filling
⅔ cup heavy cream
½ cup sugar
2 large eggs
Zest and juice of 2 lemons
3½ tablespoons unsalted butter

Make the pastry. Rub the flour and butter together with your fingertips until the mixture looks like coarse bread crumbs. (A cool kitchen and cool fingers help.) Mix in the sugar. Using a round-ended knife in a cutting motion, add the egg and water and mix until the ingredients come together into a dough ball.

Put the dough ball on a cool, floured work surface and lightly knead with the palm of your hand to ensure an evenly blended pastry. Wrap and refrigerate to rest and chill for 40 minutes.

Lightly butter a 10-inch tart pan with a removable bottom. Roll out the dough on a lightly floured surface, then line the pan. Trim the edges with a knife and refrigerate to chill and relax for 20 minutes.

Heat the oven to 375°F.

Put the cream, sugar, eggs, and lemon zest and juice into a bowl and whisk well until creamy. Melt the butter and whisk it into the lemon mixture, then pour the lemon mixture into the chilled pastry shell.

Carefully place the tart in the oven and bake for 15 minutes, then reduce the heat to 325°F. and bake for 20 minutes or until the filling has set. Cool for 1 hour before serving.

Grandmother's Festival Loaf   Serves 6

This is a lovely loaf—half bread, half cake—traditionally from the Auvergne region, hence its name, Fouace
Aveyronnaise.

½ cup milk
1 (¼-ounce) package active dry yeast
3½ tablespoons sugar, plus a pinch of sugar for the
    yeast
3 cups all-purpose flour
3½ tablespoons unsalted butter, softened
2 large eggs
1 tablespoon orange flower water or rum
⅔ cup chopped candied fruits
1 large egg, beaten, for glazing

Barely warm the milk in a small saucepan over
low heat just to remove the chill (no warmer than
115°F.). Sprinkle in the yeast and a pinch of sugar.
Let stand for a few minutes.

Place the flour, butter, remaining 3½ tablespoons sugar, 2 eggs, orange flower water, and the
yeast mixture in a large bowl and mix well. Add the
candied fruits. Turn the dough out onto a lightly
floured surface. Knead for 8 minutes.

Return the dough to the bowl, cover, and keep
in a warm place for about 1 hour. The mixture
should double in size.

Turn out the dough onto a floured surface
again and knead again until the dough is soft and
elastic. Lightly butter a baking sheet and dust it with
flour. Knock back the dough and then knead and
shape into a long sausage, join the two ends together
into a circle, place it on the baking sheet, glaze with
half of the beaten egg, and leave it to rest, covered
with a kitchen towel, for 1 hour, until double in size.

Heat the oven to 400°F. Just before placing the
loaf in the oven, glaze it with egg again. Cook for 30
minutes, until golden brown.

I find bread-making extremely therapeutic, and this
finished loaf looks beautiful, like a summer garland
studded with colorful pieces of crystallized fruit.
I like to make it on Midsummer's Eve, and eat it out
in the garden with cheese, fruit, and honey.

Breton Flan Serves 6

This typical Breton flan, *Far Breton*, is a favorite emergency dessert, and all the members of my family have a different version of it. This one belongs to Juliette Jeuland of Châteaubourg, and uses the traditional prunes, but you can also use dried apricots, cherries, berries, or raisins soaked in Armagnac.

¾ cup plus 2 tablespoons all-purpose flour
½ cup light brown sugar, plus more for sprinkling
3 large eggs
2 cups milk
5 tablespoons (¼ cup plus 1 tablespoon) unsalted
    butter, plus softened butter for the dish
5 ounces chopped pitted prunes

Heat the oven to 375°F.

Mix the flour, brown sugar, and eggs in a large bowl until smooth and blended.

Warm the milk and butter until the butter has melted, then add to the flour mixture and blend together well. Finally, stir in the prunes.

Butter a shallow baking dish, preferably earthenware, and pour in the prune mixture. Cook for 30 minutes, until risen and browned on top. Sprinkle with additional brown sugar, and serve warm or cold.

Gâteau Breton Serves 6

This is a traditional Breton cake with a rich, buttery taste and a slightly "sandy" texture, like that of the *sablé* cookies of the region. Everyone has his or her own private way of doing it. This is the plain recipe, from Danielle Stéphan of Trégastel, but you can fill your *gâteau* with raspberry jam, prunes, or liqueur-soaked fruit for a moist, luxurious version.

1½ cups all-purpose flour
2 cups sugar, preferably superfine
5 tablespoons (½ stick plus 1 tablespoon) unsalted
    butter, cut into small pieces and softened, plus
    more for the pan
5 large egg yolks
Zest of 1 orange
Milk for glazing the cake

Heat the oven to 325°F. Generously butter a 9- or 10-inch cake pan with a removable bottom insert (available at well-supplied kitchenware shops) or a springform pan.

Place the flour in a large bowl; add the sugar, butter, egg yolks, and orange zest, and work together with your fingers until all the ingredients are evenly blended—the mixture will be quite sticky. Press the mixture evenly in the prepared pan.

Make a pattern in the top of the dough with a knife or pastry cutter, and brush the surface with a little milk. Bake for 35 minutes, until the cake is golden brown and has come away from the sides of the pan.

Leave to cool in the pan for 5 minutes. Remove the cake on its base from the pan.

Serve straight from the oven, warm or cold.

Tarte Tatin Serves 6

This beautifully golden, caramelized tart is best served warm, but not too hot, so that the flavors really get a chance to develop. It is a wonderful autumn recipe for apples that hold their shape, such as Jonathans—or Pippins, if you prefer something with a little more bite.

For the pastry
1 cup plus 1 tablespoon all-purpose flour
7 tablespoons (¾ stick plus 1 tablespoon) chilled
    unsalted butter, cut into small pieces
1½ tablespoons sugar
2 large egg yolks

For the apples
½ cup sugar
3 tablespoons unsalted butter
5 apples, peeled, cored, and quartered

Make the pastry. Rub together the flour and butter with your fingertips until it resembles coarse bread crumbs. Mix in the sugar. Using a round-bladed knife in a cutting motion, add the yolks and mix until the ingredients come together into a dough ball. Turn the dough out onto a floured surface, dust your hands with a little flour, and knead briefly until the dough is evenly blended. Wrap and refrigerate to chill and rest for 30 minutes.

Make the apples. Place an 8- to 10-inch oven-proof skillet over medium heat. Add the sugar and butter and melt until syrupy.

Heat the oven to 400°F.

Arrange the apple quarters in the skillet and cook for 15 minutes; this gives the golden color to the apples and allows the sugar to turn to caramel.

Roll out the dough on a lightly floured surface to a diameter slightly wider than the skillet. Remove the skillet pan from the heat and quickly lay the dough over the apples, tucking in any excess around the edges. Place in the oven and bake for 20 minutes, then reduce the heat to 350°F. and bake for 20 minutes.

Remove from the oven and gently ease a knife all the way around the edge of the tart. Place a large heatproof plate upside down on top of the skillet and quickly turn over the pan and plate, releasing the tart onto the plate. Lift off the skillet to reveal golden brown apples and a syrupy sauce.

Hot puddings are a rarity in France, but this famous tart is one of the best. I particularly like it when it is very slightly burned, so that the caramel develops a smoky flavor and the pastry a sticky, crisp texture. It is perfect with good vanilla ice cream.

Apple Slipper   Serves 6

This little flaky butter pastry, *Chausson aux Pommes,* is named for its shape. It is a favorite with children at *goûter*, the four o'clock snack that is traditional in France. Serve it warm.

1 cup plus 2 tablespoons (2¼ sticks) chilled unsalted
    butter
1¾ cups all-purpose flour, plus extra for sprinkling
⅓ cup cold water
1 pound apples, peeled, cored, and diced
2 tablespoons sugar, plus extra for sprinkling
½ teaspoon ground cinnamon
1 large egg, beaten
Sugar, for sprinkling

Take 14 tablespoons (1¾ sticks) of the butter and cut it into very small pieces. Place the pieces on a plate and leave at room temperature to barely lose their chill for 20 minutes.

Put the flour in a bowl, add a few pieces of the butter from the plate, and toss them in the flour using a round-bladed knife. Continue adding the butter until all of it is well coated in flour, so that no pieces get the chance to clump together. Add the cold water and quickly mix with a cutting motion until the pastry comes together into a ball.

Transfer to a lightly floured, cool surface and gently shape with your hands into a brick. Roll out to an 8 × 6-inch rectangle. Fold one-third over, the other third to cover that (like folding a business letter), then use the rolling pin to press the open edges together, trapping pockets of air. Refrigerate for 5 minutes.

Lightly flour the surface again, and roll out and fold again as above. Do this three more times, refrigerating after each "turn." Wrap and refrigerate for 1 hour.

Melt the remaining 4 tablespoons (½ stick) butter in a large skillet over moderate heat, add the apples, and cook gently for 5 minutes. Stir in the sugar and cinnamon, and cool completely.

Heat the oven to 375°F.

Lightly flour a baking sheet and roll out the pastry to a ⅛-inch-thick round. Spoon the apples onto one half, brush the edges with some of the beaten egg, and fold the pastry over into a half-moon shape. Crimp the edges with your fingers to seal them. Brush with the rest of the beaten egg, pierce with a fork, and sprinkle with a little sugar. Bake for 20 minutes. Reduce the heat to 325°F and bake for 20 minutes more.

Cherry Clafoutis   Serves 6

This simple dessert can also be made with other soft fruits, such as apricots, plums, peaches, blackberries, and black currants.

1 tablespoon unsalted butter, at room temperature, for the dish
1½ pounds sweet cherries, pitted
¾ cup plus 2 tablespoons all-purpose flour
⅓ cup sugar
3 large eggs
1¼ cups milk
1 teaspoon vanilla extract
Confectioners' sugar, for serving

Heat the oven to 350°F. Butter a shallow oven-proof dish. Spread the cherries in the dish.

Put the flour and sugar in a large bowl, mix together, and make a well in the middle. In another bowl, whisk the eggs; add the milk and vanilla and whisk to combine.

Slowly pour the liquids into the dry ingredients, beating constantly until all the liquid has been added and you have a smooth batter. Pour over the cherries.

Bake for 40 minutes, until the batter is firm to the touch and golden on top. Sift with confectioners' sugar on top and serve just warm.

This is a summer favorite with children, although
the grown-up version, with the addition of kirsch,
also goes down rather well. I got this recipe from my
aunt Claudine, whose cherry trees I remember with
great affection.

Braised Cherries with Spiced Toasts   Serves 6

The French name is Soupe aux Cerises, though this is not quite what we expect from a soup.

1 pound sweet cherries, pitted
¼ cup plus 2 tablespoons sugar
1 tablespoon kirsch (optional)
5 tablespoons (½ cup plus 1 tablespoon) unsalted
    butter
10 baguette slices
1 teaspoon ground cinnamon
½ tablespoon all-purpose flour

Place the cherries, 2 tablespoons of the sugar, and the kirsch, if using, in a saucepan over medium heat. Bring to a boil, then reduce the heat and simmer for 15 minutes.

Heat the butter in a skillet and sauté the baguette slices on each side until golden.

Remove the bread, place on the bottom of a serving dish, and dust with the remaining ¼ cup sugar and the cinnamon. When the cherries are tender and cooked, remove them from the juice with a slotted spoon and pile on the bread.

Dissolve the flour with a little water to make a thin paste, and whisk it into the warm cherry juice. Gently bring to a boil. The mixture will thicken slightly, becoming velvety. Pour over the bread and cherries, and serve hot.

Chantilly Meringues   Serves 6

These light and fluffy meringues are perfect with fruit, such as a bowl of fresh summer berries or the Slow Fudge Sauce on this page, or a drizzle of chocolate fondue (page 233).

For the meringues
3 large egg whites
¾ cup plus 2 tablespoons superfine sugar

For the crème chantilly
1¼ cups heavy cream
2 tablespoons superfine sugar
Few drops of vanilla extract

Heat the oven to 275°F. Line a baking sheet with parchment paper.

Put the egg whites in a bowl and whisk rapidly until stiff, using an electric mixer. Whisk in half of the sugar, then whisk in the remaining sugar. Scoop 12 spoonfuls of the meringue mixture onto the parchment paper. Bake for 2 hours. For perfectly crisp meringues, leave the meringues to dry in the turned-off oven for an additional 12 hours.

Whisk the cream with the sugar and vanilla until it stands in soft peaks. Scoop cream on to six of the meringues, then sandwich the other six meringues on top of these. Chill before serving.

Slow Fudge Sauce   Serves 6

This tantalizingly slow fudge sauce—*Caramel Marie Sorin*, from my great-aunt Marinette—is a luxury for those days when ice cream alone just isn't enough. Part of the pleasure of this recipe is the time it takes to prepare it and the anticipation that goes with it. By the time it is ready, the entire house smells like a sweet shop, spirits have magically lifted, and even the rain has stopped. If you have some left (this has never happened to me yet), then line a pan with parchment paper, pour in the sauce, and leave it to set in the refrigerator for a couple of hours. Then cut into squares for a smooth and creamy fudge.

2½ cups sugar
1 (14-ounce) can sweetened condensed milk
⅓ cup whole milk
1 tablespoon unsalted butter

Put the sugar, condensed milk, whole milk, and butter in a heavy-bottomed saucepan and cook over very low heat, stirring constantly, until all the sugar has melted. You must stir constantly, otherwise the sugar will burn and the sauce becomes inedible. Slowly bring to a boil, and simmer very gently for 20 minutes, continuing to stir all the while.

Remove from the heat and beat well with a wooden spoon until the sauce is golden thick and smooth. Serve warm with a really good vanilla ice cream.

Crème Brûlée Serves 6

This is a quick and easy version of a perennial favorite—try adding a handful of red currants or raspberries to the mixture for a fresh, summery variation. Make this a day before serving it to get a really firm set.

1 vanilla bean
1½ cups heavy cream
5 large egg yolks
2 tablespoons granulated sugar
Confectioners' sugar, for topping

Cut the vanilla bean in half lengthways, then scrape out the seeds into a small saucepan with the cream. Discard the bean. Gently bring the cream to a simmer—do not boil—then remove from the heat.

Heat the oven to 325°F.

In a heatproof bowl, beat together the egg yolks and granulated sugar until light and fluffy. Stir in the vanilla cream and mix well. Place the bowl over a saucepan of simmering water over low heat, stirring constantly, until the mixture coats the back of the spoon, about 8 minutes. Pour the custard into 6 individual ramekins (or you could use one large baking dish).

Make a bain-marie with a deep roasting pan: place the ramekins in the pan and half-fill the pan with hot water. Place the pan in the oven and cook the custards for 20 minutes. Remove the ramekins from the water and allow to cool, then refrigerate overnight.

The next day, preheat the broiler. Sift an even layer of the confectioners' sugar over the custards and place under the broiler. The sugar will melt and caramelize. Move the dishes as needed so that they brown evenly. Cool completely before serving.

Crème Caramel Serves 6

This is one of my favorite desserts. No two people make it in exactly the same way, but this is my grandmother's recipe, and ideally it should be made 24 hours in advance to give the rich caramel color at the bottom of the dish time to develop.

For the caramel
1 cup superfine or granulated sugar
3 tablespoons water

For the cream
2 cups milk
3 large eggs
2 large egg yolks
⅓ cup superfine or granulated sugar
Few drops of vanilla extract

Heat the oven to 325°F. Place a soufflé dish in the oven to warm.

Make the caramel. Place the sugar and water in a small skillet. Bring to a boil, then simmer until golden brown. Remove the dish from the oven, and pour the caramel into the soufflé dish.

Make the cream. Place the milk in a saucepan and bring gently to a boil. Remove from the heat. Mix the eggs, egg yolks, sugar, and vanilla in a bowl. Stir in the hot milk and mix well. Strain the mixture through a fine sieve into the caramel-lined soufflé dish.

Place the soufflé dish in a deep roasting pan and half-fill the pan with hot water. Carefully place in the oven and cook for 1 hour. Remove the dish from the water and cool. Refrigerate for at least 1 hour before serving (or chill overnight).

To unmold the custard, run a knife around the inside of the dish. Place a deep serving platter on top and invert the dish and the platter together. Carefully remove the dish, and serve.

Kirsch Soufflé   Serves 6

Soufflé means "blown," like glass. People tend to think that soufflés are delicate and tricky to make, but this isn't true. It's a quick, light, versatile dish—just avoid opening the oven door while your soufflé is cooking, and eat it right away. This shouldn't be a problem—it's irresistible!

2 tablespoons unsalted butter, plus softened butter
    for the dish
9 tablespoons sugar, preferably superfine
⅓ cup all-purpose flour
⅔ cup plus ¼ cup milk
4 large egg yolks
½ cup kirsch
7 large egg whites, at room temperature
Confectioners' sugar for sifting

Heat the oven to 375°F.

Lightly rub the inside of an 8-inch soufflé dish with a little butter. Add 2 tablespoons of the sugar, and roll the dish around until evenly coated with the sugar; tap out the excess sugar.

Place the flour in a bowl, add ¼ cup of the milk, and work to form a smooth paste.

Heat the remaining ⅔ cup milk, 7 tablespoons sugar, and 2 tablespoons butter in a saucepan. When this reaches a boil, slowly whisk it into the flour paste, whisking until the mixture is smooth. Return the milk mixture to the saucepan and bring to a boil, stirring constantly. Remove from the heat and add the egg yolks and kirsch, mixing well until smooth.

Beat the egg whites in a large bowl with an electric mixer until stiff. Add the kirsch mixture to the whites and fold in quickly until evenly blended. Carefully pour into the prepared dish, put immediately into the oven, and bake for 10 minutes.

Slide the soufflé on the oven rack out of the oven, quickly sift the top with confectioners' sugar, and bake for another 5 minutes. Serve immediately on warmed plates.

Note: If you wish, bake the soufflés in six buttered-and-sugared individual ramekins. They will take slightly less time to bake.

There are plenty of variations for this easy dish. Try using Grand Marnier, chartreuse, or rum for a change, and serve with a sweet, fruity wine such as Sauternes or Monbazillac.

Ripe pears just off the tree have almost nothing in common with the hard, green ones you find in some supermarkets. Choose a firm, slightly mushy species (such as Bosc), which will really absorb the flavors of the wine and spices.

Pears Poached in Red Wine Serves 6

Poires au Vin Rouge is a terrific way of preparing autumn pears, and fills the house with a marvelous scent of wine and spices. The juice makes a wonderful spicy punch—just add a little cognac!

1 (750-milliliter) bottle red Burgundy wine
½ cup sugar, preferably superfine
4 whole cloves
2 blades of mace
6 firm-ripe pears, such as Bosc

Place the wine, sugar, cloves, and mace in a saucepan large enough also to accommodate the pears and gently bring to a simmer.

Peel the pears, carefully keeping their beautiful shape and the stems on. Add the pears to the wine and simmer for 30 minutes, turning the pears to ensure even cooking and staining from the red wine. Cool the pears in the wine.

Serve the pears at room temperature. The pears can be served on their own or in a soup bowl with a ladleful of the red wine.

Pear and Chocolate Brioche Pudding Serves 6

Brioche is a lovely soft roll or loaf made from a yeast dough enriched with eggs and butter, which give it its distinctive color and flavor. Brioche varies in shape from region to region, with the Parisian variety—a small ball of brioche on top of a larger base, or *brioche à tête*—perhaps most familiar to us. The most highly regarded brioches come from Gournay and Gisors in Normandy. Serve with scoops of vanilla ice cream for a melt-in-your-mouth dessert.

Softened butter, for the dish
11 ounces brioche, sliced
5 ripe pears, peeled and sliced
2 cups light cream or half-and-half
1¼ cups milk
3½ ounces bittersweet (70 percent cocoa) chocolate
¼ cup sugar, preferably superfine, plus more for
    sprinkling
3 large eggs

Butter a shallow baking dish. Arrange the sliced brioche and pears alternately in the dish.

Warm the cream and milk in a saucepan over low heat. Chop the chocolate into small pieces, add it to the warm milk along with the sugar, and stir until melted. Do not boil. Whisk the eggs and mix them into the warm chocolate milk, then pour the liquid over the brioche and pear slices, being sure to moisten the brioche. Press down with a spatula, and leave to stand for 40 minutes.

Heat the oven to 325°F.

Sprinkle the pudding with a little extra sugar, and place it in a bain-marie (that is, place the baking dish in a large roasting pan and fill the pan with hot water to come halfway up the pudding dish). Place in the oven and cook for 45 minutes, until soft and golden.

Polenta Pudding Cake Serves 6

This warm polenta-based pudding cake, *Gâteau Francesca,* is lovely cold-weather comfort food.

1 cup plus 2 tablespoons (2¼ sticks) unsalted
　　butter, softened, plus more for the dish
1¼ cups sugar, preferably superfine
3 lemons, preferably organic
4 large eggs
¾ cup polenta
¼ cup (1 ounce) ground almonds (use a food
　　processor)
¾ cup all-purpose flour
Heavy cream, to serve

Heat the oven to 350°F. Lightly butter an 8-inch pie plate.

In a large bowl, cream together the butter and sugar with an electric mixer until smooth. Finely grate the lemon zest from 2½ lemons and then juice the lemons. Add the zest and juice to the creamed butter and mix. Thinly slice the remaining ½ lemon and reserve. Beat in the eggs—the mixture will curdle, but do not worry, this is normal. Then beat in the polenta and ground almonds. Finally, fold in the flour with a large spoon.

Transfer the batter to the pie plate, arrange the lemon slices on top, and bake for 25 to 30 minutes. Serve warm, with a pitcher of cream for pouring.

Mémée's Cherries

Of all my great-grandmother's recipes, this is the one I remember best. She gave my mother several jars of these preserved cherries when my mother came to England, and there are still some left, a precious few, at the bottom of the liqueur cabinet. On special occasions we drink a little of the liqueur, with a single cherry at the bottom of the glass. The cherries are forty years old now, and they have macerated for so long that even the pits—and the little kernel inside—are infused with the flavor of the Armagnac. You can use the same basic recipe for almost any fruit: raspberries, small plums, blackberries, red currants. You can vary the alcohol, too; any kind of clear spirit works well, including vodka or white rum. I make my own now, although I still like Mémée's best. Perhaps in another forty years . . .

Basic ingredients for the amount of your choice
Sour cherries
Armagnac
Superfine sugar
Pinch of ground cinnamon
you also need a clean glass canning jar with a lid

Choose undamaged sour cherries of very good quality. Wash the cherries and leave the pits in. Cut off part of the stem with scissors.

Put three layers of cherries in the bottom of the jar. Top with 2 to 3 tablespoons of sugar. Add a pinch of cinnamon. Repeat this process until you are close to the top of the jar, then cover with a layer of sugar about ¾ inch thick. Top with Armagnac so that the fruit is covered. Tighten the lid. Turn the jar a few times to dissolve the sugar.

Store in a cool, dark place. Turn again in a few days' time.

Consume after a few months (the longer you wait, the better the result).

Sloe Gin and Mango Crush   Serves 6

This makes a delicious and wickedly refreshing end to a rich meal.

3 large ripe mangoes
3 tablespoons gin
3 tablespoons sloe gin
2 ounces bittersweet (70 percent cocoa) chocolate,
    cut into 6 pieces

Place six tall glasses in the freezer.

Peel the skin away from each mango with a sharp knife, then cut all the flesh away from the pit and roughly chop it. Place it in the bowl of a blender (or in a bowl with a hand-held blender) and puree. Add the gin and sloe gin and mix well. Pour into a shallow metal pan.

Freeze for 1 hour and then remove and break up the ice crystals with a fork. Return to the freezer and freeze for 10 minutes before again breaking up the crystals with a fork.

Repeat this process at least five or six times, or until the crystals are firm enough to hold their shape. Fill the chilled glasses with the crush and place in the refrigerator for 10 minutes. Serve at once with a small chunk of chocolate.

My brother came up with this delicious and unusual dessert—so simple and yet so good! My daughter prefers the alcohol-free version, topped with a cherry and curls of milk chocolate.

Chocolate

I have to admit that for a while after writing *Chocolat* I felt that I would never be able to eat chocolate again. After months of chocolate festivals, chocolate premières, chocolate factories, chocolate-themed parties and openings and dinners; after being on the set of the film, where even the wood shavings smelled of chocolate, I think even the most devoted chocolate addict might have begun to feel rather sated. I was disgusted, chocced-out, finished.

The Italians saved me; as I arrived at yet another chocolate event, this time in the exquisite coffee shop and chocolaterie of Cova, in Milan, I was greeted by the owner, who, taking one look at my pale, exhausted face, smiled and said, "Wait here. I have something special for you to try." As he vanished into a back room, I tried to school my features (for the thousandth time) into an expression of blissful surprise: Chocolate! My favorite!

I felt my worst suspicions about to be confirmed when the gentleman returned carrying a silver tray—which on closer examination revealed a generous pile of the most incredible, delicious, vocabulary-challengingly excellent anchovy crostini I have ever eaten. I spent that blissful afternoon gorging on anchovy crostini and plump black olives, and when I got home again I found that my chocolate aversion had magically disappeared. I was cured.

As a result, when we were compiling this book we found that the chocolate recipes outnumbered the rest to such an extent that we decided to create an entirely separate chapter devoted to this uniquely versatile and enchanting substance. Some of the recipes are from *Chocolat*—the ones you keep asking me for—and some are old (or new) favorites gathered along the way.

To my great disappointment, the gentleman from Cova refused to give me the recipe for his lifesaving anchovy crostini, but you can make a good approximation by using the tapenade recipe on page 59.

Chocolate: a unique substance. It can be melted, grated, sculpted, and spun. It can be eaten in savories as well as sweets with equal pleasure, or just devoured on its own. Bliss.

Tempering Chocolate

Note for all chocolate-lovers: never store chocolate or chill dipped chocolate confections in the refrigerator.

Couverture is also called dipping or coating chocolate, and professional chocolate makers always use it. It comes in all varieties (milk, bittersweet, and white), but has a high cocoa butter content, thus making it ideal for hand-made chocolates. The best couverture comes from France, Belgium, and Switzerland.

Couverture needs to be tempered in order to give it a perfectly smooth and glossy finish. Tempering is really very simple, and although it takes a little time, it is worth the effort to achieve a really professional gloss. You will need an instant-read thermometer, and then all the process requires is to take the couverture up to a certain temperature and cool it, then reheat it slightly to a workable dipping texture. This changes the crystalline structure of the chocolate and makes it shiny and manageable.

If the idea of tempering chocolate really doesn't appeal, you can simply melt good-quality eating chocolate using the double-boiler method. It tastes fine, although your chocolate will not have the shiny, professional texture or the "snap" of tempered couverture.

To temper chocolate:

Chop the chocolate (preferably couverture) into small pieces. If it comes from a professional supplier, it may already come as buttons.

Place the chocolate in a heatproof steel bowl. Stand the dish over a saucepan of simmering water over low heat, and melt, stirring occasionally, until the chocolate reaches 115° to 120°F. on the thermometer. Remove the dish from the saucepan and stand it in a shallow pan of cold water. Mix well and allow the temperature to drop back to 80°F.—the melted chocolate will thicken somewhat.

Finally, return the dish to the simmering water, mix well, and heat the chocolate to 88° to 90°F., where it will be shiny and fluid enough for dipping.

The chocolate has now been tempered and is ready for use.

Mendiants Makes about 65

These are my own favorites—little disks of
chocolate sprinkled with whatever you like best:
almonds, candied lemon peel, glacéed cherries,
walnuts, or fat Malaga raisins. Anouchka likes to do
the artistic part (while I do most of the eating). The
name means "beggars." Traditionally served at
Christmas with toppings of dried fruit and nuts in
four colors, they were meant to represent the four
Roman Catholic mendicant orders (white for the
Dominicans, gray for the Franciscans, brown for the
Carmelites, and deep purple for the Augustines).

18 ounces milk or bittersweet (70 percent cocoa)
    chocolate couverture, tempered as on page 216
5 ounces of your combined choice of almonds, wal-
    nuts, raisins, golden raisins, candied fruits

Place teaspoonfuls of the tempered couverture
on a large sheet of parchment paper. Gently spread
each one with the back of the spoon to make 1-inch
wide disks. Scatter the fruits and nuts on top of the
disks and allow to cool.

Apricot Truffles Makes about 36

The slight sharpness of the apricot provides a
delicious contrast to the dark chocolate in these
luscious truffles.

1 pound bittersweet (70 percent cocoa) chocolate
⅔ cup milk
1 tablespoon apricot liqueur
12 soft dried apricots, finely diced
7 ounces milk chocolate couverture
1 cup cocoa powder

Chop the bittersweet chocolate into small
pieces and melt in a heatproof bowl over a saucepan
of simmering water. Heat the milk in a small
saucepan until boiling. Pour into the melted chocolate and stir well. Add the liqueur and blend until
smooth.

Remove from the heat. Gradually add the apricot pieces, stirring constantly. Cool until the mixture thickens and forms a workable paste. Roll the
paste into balls between your fingers. Leave to cool
completely while you temper the milk chocolate
couverture for dipping (see page 216).

Sift the cocoa powder onto a plate. Using a thin
fork, stab the truffles one at a time and dip in the
tempered milk chocolate. Transfer to a large sheet
of parchment paper to cool until almost set. Roll the
truffles in the cocoa powder and leave to cool completely. Repeat with all the truffles.

Left to right are untipped Nipples of Venus, Mendiants, finished Nipples of Venus (page 220), and Apricot Truffles. For a shortcut version of the truffles, don't bother with the couverture and simply roll the truffles in cocoa powder.

Nipples of Venus   Makes about 70

This was originally an Italian confection, but I put it in because I couldn't resist the name.

For the filling
8 ounces bittersweet (70 percent cocoa) chocolate
1¼ cups heavy cream

For dippng
3½ ounces bittersweet (70 percent cocoa) chocolate, preferably couverture
2 ounces white chocolate

For the filling, chop the chocolate into small pieces and melt in a heatproof bowl over a saucepan of simmering water. Heat the cream in a small saucepan and add to the melted chocolate, mixing until evenly blended. Leave to cool for 2 hours. Then, using an electric mixer, beat until the mixture becomes stiff and holds its shape.

Line three baking sheets with parchment paper. Put the chocolate mixture into a pastry bag fitted with a ½-inch plain tip. Pipe little mounds—or nipples—onto the parchment paper. Refrigerate to chill and set.

For dipping, temper the bittersweet chocolate (see page 216). Take each nipple and dip in the tempered chocolate, reheating the chocolate as necessary to return it to a dipping viscosity. Return to the parchment paper and leave to set for an hour.

Melt the white chocolate in a heatproof bowl over simmering water. Take each nipple and dip the tip into the white chocolate. Enjoy!

Chocolate Pot

This is pure indulgence of the highest order. Try adding finely grated orange zest, or a dash of brandy, whisky, or Kahlua, to make your own personal pot.

9 ounces bittersweet (70 percent cocoa) chocolate
3 cups heavy cream
6 chocolate scrolls or 6 teaspoons crème fraîche, for serving

Chop the chocolate into small pieces and melt in a heatproof bowl over a saucepan of simmering water. Heat the cream in a saucepan until just simmering, then add to the chocolate and blend until a smooth thick sauce has formed.

Pour into small ramekins or glasses and refrigerate overnight. Garnish with a chocolate scroll or a teaspoon of crème fraîche.

This is Lawrence's chocolate cake, a cake so rich you can serve it only in slivers! Always line the pan with baking parchment (not waxed paper) to ensure you can easily release this rich, moist cake.

Gâteau Lawrence   Serves 6

This is a rich cake. If you find, as I do, that the chocolate icing seems a little too much of a good thing, try drizzling about 6 tablespoons of warmed apricot jam over the cake just before serving—the sharp tang of the fruit makes a wonderful contrast to the dark chocolate. Bliss!

For the cake

6½ ounces bittersweet (70 percent cocoa) chocolate
12 tablespoons (1½ sticks) unsalted butter, at room temperature
⅔ cup sugar
1⅔ cups (7 ounces) ground sliced almonds (grind in a food processor or blender)
4 large eggs, separated

For the icing

3½ ounces bittersweet (70 percent cocoa) chocolate
3 tablespoons unsalted butter

Heat the oven to 300°F. Line a 10-inch spring-form pan with parchment paper.

Chop the chocolate into small pieces and melt it in a heatproof bowl over a saucepan of simmering water. Remove from the heat and cool until tepid.

Cream together the butter and sugar until soft and creamy using an electric mixer. Add the ground almonds, egg yolks, and melted chocolate, and beat until evenly blended.

Whisk the egg whites until stiff, add to the cake mixture, and quickly fold in until evenly mixed using a rubber spatula. Pour into the prepared pan and bake for 35 minutes. A light crust will form on the top and the middle should still be a little squishy. Leave to cool a little before carefully removing the sides. Cool on a wire rack. Slide a long knife under the cake to release it from the parchment, but leave the cake on the paper.

For the icing, melt the chocolate and butter in a heatproof bowl over a saucepan of simmering water. Spread evenly over the top of the cake and leave to set. Slide the cake off the parchment paper onto a serving platter.

My brother Lawrence discovered this luscious chocolate cake, which uses ground almonds instead of flour for an incredibly moist and gooey consistency.

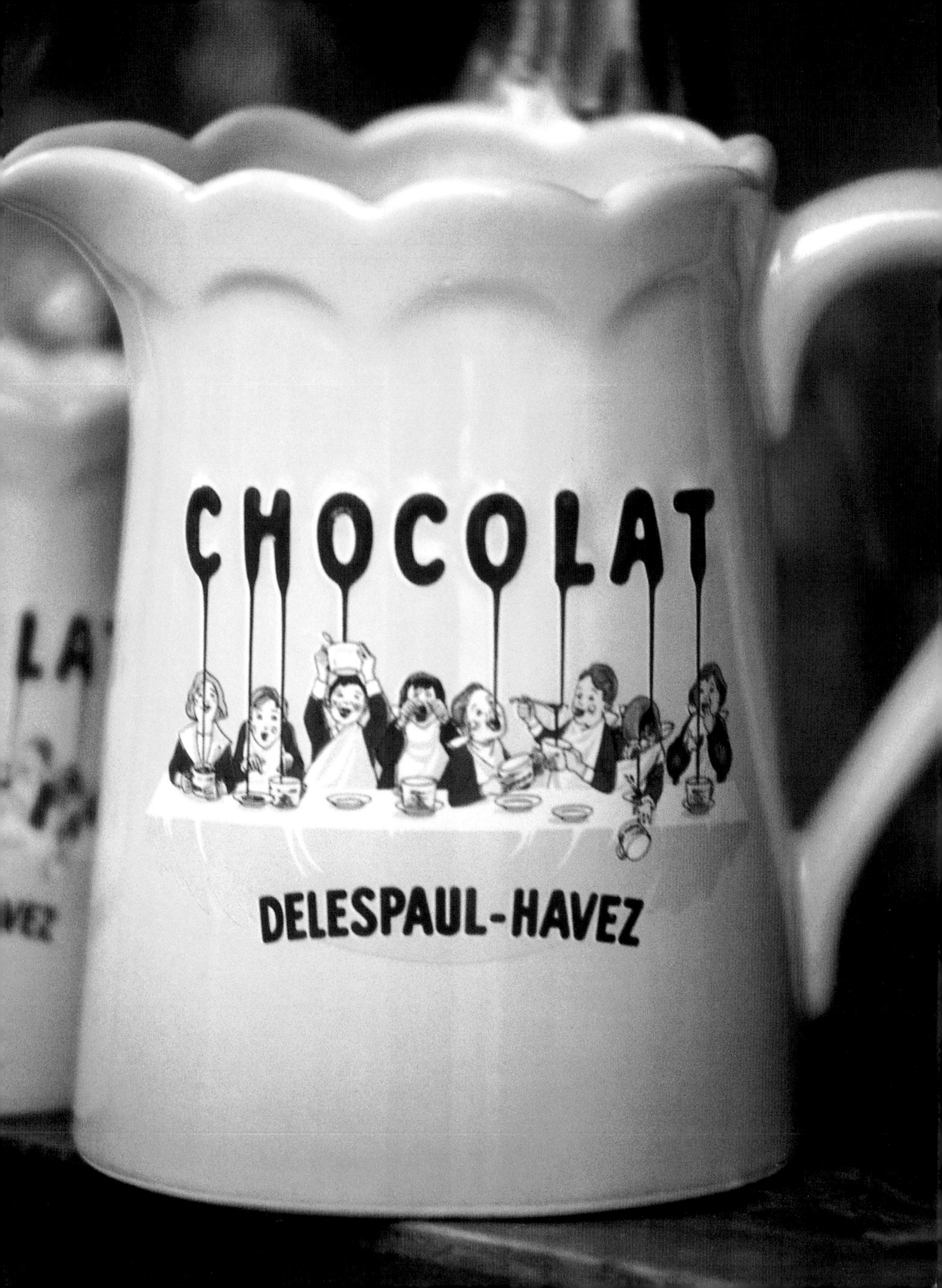
CHOCOLAT
DELESPAUL-HAVEZ

Anouchka's Chocolate Cake   Serves 6

My daughter usually prefers fresh mangoes to chocolate, but sometimes makes an exception in the case of this very special two-chocolate cake.

For the cake
½ ounces bittersweet (70 percent cocoa) chocolate
½ tablespoon butter, at room temperature, plus extra for the pan
¾ cup brown sugar
3 eggs
⅓ cup ground almonds (grind in a food processor or blender)
1 cup self-rising flour

For the icing
1½ cups unrefined icing sugar
2 tablespoons unsalted butter, at room temperature, cut into pieces
¼ cup hot milk, as needed
⅓ cup cocoa powder
1 ounce white chocolate, grated
1 ounce bittersweet chocolate, grated

For the cake, heat the oven to 350°F. Butter an 8-inch springform cake pan.

Melt the chocolate in a heatproof bowl over a pan of simmering water. Cool the chocolate to tepid. Cream together the butter and sugar with an electric mixer until creamy and fluffy. Break the eggs into the butter and sugar one at a time and beat. The mixture will curdle, but don't worry—it will come back once you add the flour. Add the melted chocolate and ground almonds and blend well. Fold in the flour with a large metal spoon, then transfer the mixture to the cake pan.

Bake for 35 minutes, or until the cake has come away from the sides of the pan, or a knife inserted into it comes out clean. Allow the cake to cool in the pan for 5 minutes before turning out onto a cake rack. Then cool completely before icing it.

To make the icing, sift the icing sugar into a bowl, add the butter pieces and mix with a fork. In a separate small bowl, pour the milk over the cocoa powder and mix until dissolved, then add this to the icing sugar and blend. Spread over the cake and let stand to cool and set. Decorate with the grated white and bittersweet chocolate.

Roulade Bicolore Serves 6

This two-tone cake combines two kinds of chocolate for a melting contrast of flavors. Topped with chocolate curls, it makes a spectacular Yule log or celebration cake.

For the roulade
2¼ ounces bittersweet (70 percent cocoa) chocolate
3 tablespoons unsalted butter, at room temperature
⅓ cup packed light brown sugar
2 large eggs, at room temperature
2 tablespoons milk, at room temperature
1 tablespoon coffee liqueur, such as Kahlua
¾ cup plus 2 tablespoons self-rising flour

For the filling
1 cup heavy cream
4½ ounces white chocolate, grated
½ teaspoon vanilla extract

For the decoration
1 ounce white chocolate, grated
1 ounce bittersweet (70 percent cocoa)
    chocolate, grated

Heat the oven to 350°F. Line a 15 × 10-inch jelly-roll pan with parchment paper.

First make the roulade: Chop the chocolate into small pieces and melt in a heatproof bowl over a saucepan of simmering water. Remove from the heat and cool until tepid.

Place the butter and brown sugar in a bowl and beat until creamy and fluffy using an electric mixer. Add the eggs and continue to beat—the mixture could curdle but this is normal. Pour in the chocolate and mix well. Add the milk and liqueur, and mix until smooth. Fold in the flour, then spread the mixture in the prepared pan. Bake for 10 minutes. Take the cake out of the pan and leave to cool on a wire rack.

Make the filling: Whisk the cream until it stands in very soft peaks using an electric mixer. Lightly mix in the white chocolate and vanilla. Take care not to overwhip the cream or it will lose its light, soft texture. Place the cooled roulade on the work surface, parchment side down, and spread the filling on top, keeping a space clear all around the edge.

Use the parchment paper to help you roll up the roulade into a log, peeling off the paper as you go. The cake will crack slightly, but don't worry. Wrap the paper around the roulade and shape it with your hands into a smooth log, allow to sit for 5 minutes, then slide onto a serving plate, removing the paper. Decorate with the grated white and bittersweet chocolate.

A roulade is a marvelous thing, but difficult to serve. A serrated knife is likely to break it up, so use a sharp thin knife to cut it, and a metal spatula to help to hold it together.

Chocolate Cheesecake Serves 6

It takes willpower to wait out the three-hour chilling time for this exceptional cheesecake—I find that I need an extra package of those chocolate chip cookies to help me through it.

1½ cups finely crushed chocolate chip cookies
    (7 ounces)
6 tablespoons (¾ stick) unsalted butter, melted
½ teaspoon ground cinnamon
3½ ounces bittersweet (70 percent cocoa) chocolate
8 ounces crème fraîche
⅓ cup light brown sugar
¾ cup plus 2 tablespoons heavy cream
1 tablespoon coffee liqueur, such as Kahlua
3½ ounces white chocolate, grated
1 vanilla bean, split lengthwise and seeds scraped out

Put the crushed cookies in a bowl, add the melted butter and cinnamon, mix well, and press evenly into a lightly buttered 8-inch springform pan. Refrigerate until firm.

Chop the chocolate and melt in a heatproof bowl over a pan of simmering water. Remove from the heat and cool until tepid.

Beat together the crème fraîche and brown sugar until blended, then add the heavy cream and mix just until smooth. Do not beat until the crème fraîche forms peaks. Divide the mixture evenly into two bowls. Stir the melted chocolate and coffee liqueur into one bowl and the grated white chocolate and vanilla seeds into the other, just until combined.

Spoon dollops of the two mixtures onto the cookie crust and lightly mix with a fork to obtain a marbled effect. Chill for 3 hours before serving.

A truly special dessert: rich, dense, and fragrant. The marbled effect is easy to achieve, and for an even more spectacular result, decorate with chocolate curls or chocolate rose leaves.

Easy Chocolate Ice Cream
Serves 6

This grown-up chocolate ice cream, *Glace "Express" au Chocolat*, is from Janick Gestin of Laillé. Serve with your favorite toppings: chocolate curls, *crème chantilly* (whipped cream), iced Kahlua, or toasted almonds.

5½ ounces bittersweet (70 percent cocoa) chocolate
    or milk chocolate
1 cup milk
2 tablespoons coffee liqueur, such as Kahlua
1 large egg plus 2 large egg yolks
⅓ cup plus 1 tablespoon sugar, preferably superfine
1 teaspoon cornstarch
1⅓ cups heavy cream

Chop the chocolate and place in a saucepan with the milk and liqueur. Set over low heat and stir until the chocolate has melted. Remove from the heat.

Place the egg and egg yolks with the sugar and cornstarch in a heatproof bowl and beat until creamy and fluffy using an electric mixer. Pour in the melted chocolate and whisk well. Place over a saucepan of simmering water and stir constantly until it begins to thicken (10 to 15 minutes). Remove from the heat and allow to cool until tepid.

Pour the heavy cream into a bowl and whisk until it stands in soft peaks, then fold it into the chocolate mixture.

If you have an ice cream machine, use it from here. If not, transfer the ice cream to a shallow metal pan and leave in the freezer for 1 hour. Remove, beat the ice cream until smooth, and return it to the freezer. Repeat a few times until the ice cream has small crystals and can retain a good shape.

Chocolate Fondue

I love the informality of fondues and the picnic atmosphere they create. This sweet, light version is a perfect way to end a cheerful, noisy party. Use sweet almond oil if you can find it, but you can also make a good chocolate fondue without it.

For the fondue
10½ ounces bittersweet (70 percent cocoa) chocolate
6 tablespoons (¾ stick) heavy cream, heated to
    simmering
1 tablespoon cognac
1 tablespoon sweet almond oil (optional)

For dipping
Strawberries, apricot halves, pear slices, banana slices,
    peach slices, mandarin segments, or small pieces
    of sponge cake

Chop the chocolate, put into heatproof dish, and melt over a saucepan of simmering water. Then add the cream, cognac, and almond oil, if using, and stir to make a glossy sauce for dipping. Transfer to a fondue pot and keep warm as the pot requires (a votive candle works well). Serve the fondue at the table with dipping forks and all the dipping ingredients.

Chocolate Meringues   Serves 6

These luscious meringues are wonderful with crème chantilly and fresh fruit.

For the meringues
3 large egg whites, at room temperature
¾ cup plus 2 tablespoons superfine sugar
¼ cup cocoa powder, sifted

For the **crème chantilly**
1¼ cups heavy cream
2 tablespoons superfine sugar
1 tablespoon coffee liqueur, such as Kahlua

Heat the oven to 275°F. Line a baking sheet with parchment paper.

Put the egg whites in a bowl and whisk rapidly until stiff, using an electric mixer. Add the sugar and whisk rapidly for another minute. Add the cocoa powder and whisk just until blended.

Scoop 12 spoonfuls of the meringue mixture onto the parchment paper. Bake for 2 hours. For perfectly crisp meringues, leave the meringues to dry in the turned-off oven for an additional 12 hours.

For the *crème chantilly*, whisk the cream a little, add the sugar and liqueur, and continue to whisk carefully just until it stands in soft peaks. Sandwich the meringues together with the whipped cream and serve immediately.

These beautiful meringues are a feature of many elegant French pâtisseries, like fluffy caramel-colored clouds above the multicolored fruit tarts and sculptural *pièces montées*.

Long before chocolate came to us from South America,
the Aztecs drank an infusion of cacao spiced with
pepper and chile as part of their religious ceremonies.
Later, as drinking chocolate gained popularity in
Europe, sugar and milk were added to sweeten the
bitter taste, and the strong spices were no longer
needed to make it palatable.

Vianne's Spiced Hot Chocolate   Serves 2

Chile may have lost favor as an ingredient in chocolate dishes in Europe, but for me this sweet, spiced version of hot chocolate is the best morning drink: rich, dark, and invigorating enough to keep me going until lunchtime.

1⅔ cups milk
½ vanilla bean, cut in half lengthwise
½ cinnamon stick
1 hot red chile, halved and seeded
3½ ounces bittersweet (70 percent) chocolate
Brown sugar to taste (optional)
Whipped cream, chocolate curls, cognac, or
    Amaretto, to serve

Place the milk in a saucepan, add the vanilla bean, cinnamon stick, and chile, and gently bring it to a shivering simmer for 1 minute. Grate the chocolate and whisk it in until it melts. If you must, then add brown sugar, but do try without it. Take off the heat and allow it to infuse for 10 minutes, then remove the vanilla, cinnamon, and chile. Return to the heat and bring gently back to a simmer. Serve in mugs topped with whipped cream, chocolate curls, or a dash of cognac or Amaretto.

Index

RESTAURANT
BRASSERIE
DU SILLON
Spécialité de Fruits de Mer
et de Poissons
Ouvert toute l'Année

Acknowledgments

The French kitchen is a sociable place where anybody can help out, whether they are doing the cooking, preparing the vegetables, or simply telling stories to help the others pass the time. Heartfelt thanks to the many, many people who contributed ideas, recipes, photographs, and all the other ingredients that make up this book, especially photographer Debi Treloar, designer Kenneth Carroll, jacket illustrator Stuart Haygarth and jacket designer Claire Ward, art director Liz Laczynska, editors Alison Tulett, Mari Roberts, and Francesca Liversidge, and Warrior Maidens Serafina Clarke and Jennifer Luithlen. Thanks also to everyone who contributed ideas and recipes, including all the members of the Payen and Sorin families, Joanne's mother, Jeannette Payen Short, Joanne's brother Lawrence, Jean and Simone Sorin, Claudine Pénisson, Denise Douazan, and Mikaël Quaireau. Many thanks, too, to Marité and André Roty, Monique and Hamadi Kachkachi, Josette and Jacques Crochet, Juliette and Joseph Jeuland, Pierre and Janick Gestin, and Danielle and Michel Stéphan for all their help and their generous hospitality to our team during their stay in France.

We would like to thank Vicki Keppel-Compton and Laura Lenox Conyngham for recipe testing, and Vicki for assisting on the recipe shoot; Helen Trent for styling; and the following generous suppliers and hospitable hosts in both England and France.

The French House
78 York Street
London W1H 1DP
020 7298 6189
www.thefrench-house.com

M & C Vegetables
Turnham Green Terrace
London W4 1RG
020 8995 0140
www.m-and-c.co.uk

Mortimer and Bennet Deli
Turnham Green Terrace
London W4 1RG
020 8995 4145

Covent Garden
    Fishmongers
Turnham Green Terrace
London W4 1RG
020 8995 9273

Macken Brothers Butchers
Turnham Green Terrace
London W4 1RG
020 8994 2646

Farmers' markets
everywhere: see
www.farmersmarkets.net

Chalmers & Grey
    Fishmongers
67 Notting Hill Gate
London W11 3JS
020 7221 6177

Paul Bakery
115 Marylebone High Street
London W1U 4SB
020 7836 3304

Eurostar (UK) Limited
Waterloo Station
London SE1 8SE
08705 186 186
eurostar.com

Brittany Ferries
0870 5 360 360
www.brittanyferries.com

Aux Crus de Bourgogne
3 rue Bachaumont
75002 Paris
01 42 33 48 24

La Fromagerie 31
64 rue de Seine
75006 Paris
01 43 26 50 31

E. Dehillerin
18 et 20 rue Coquillière
75001 Paris
01 42 36 53 13

Hotel Aviatic
105 rue de Vaugirard
75006 Paris
01 53 63 25 50

Da Rosa
Epicurie Fine
62 rue de Seine
75006 Paris
01 40 51 00 09

Gerrard Judd
La Castafiore
51 rue St Louis en L'Île
75004 Paris

Segolene & Charles de
    Valbray
Château de Saint Patern
72610 Saint Patern
02 33 27 54 71
www.chateau-
saintpaterne.com

Marquis et Marquise
    Gicquel des Touches
Château de Sarceaux
61250 Valframbert
02 33 28 85 11
www.chateauxcountry.com
/chateaux/sarceaux

Special Dedication

Given that my role in all this has been one of maximum enjoyment and minimum effort, I am donating my share of the proceeds to the humanitarian organization Médecins Sans Frontières, who are unique among aid charities in that they are entirely secular, non-judgmental and one hundred percent committed to helping the sick and the afflicted wherever they are and regardless of race, religion, or political affiliation. This book is dedicated to them, and to everyone who has not yet discovered the pleasures of their own kitchen—what are you waiting for?

—Joanne Harris

Médecins Sans Frontières

Providing emergency medical relief to populations in danger

When an epidemic rages out of control, when a rain of shells reduces a town to ruins, when an area of conflict is too dangerous for most aid agencies to enter, MSF's skilled medical teams are there.

Médecins Sans Frontières (MSF) is the leading non-governmental organization for emergency medical aid. We provide independent medical relief to victims of war, disasters and epidemics in over eighty countries around the world, treating those who need it most, regardless of ethnic origin, religion or political affiliation.

Initially founded in Paris in 1971, MSF has become an international organization with support offices in 20 countries. Every year MSF sends around 2,500 volunteer doctors, nurses and technical support staff to some of the most far flung regions of the world to care for those most in need.

To get access to, and care for, those most vulnerable, MSF must remain scrupulously independent of governments as well as of religious and economic powers. We rely on private individuals for the majority of our funding.

You can contact us at:
Médecins Sans Frontières (UK)
67-74 Saffron Hill
London EC1N 8QX

Tel: 020 7404 6600
Fax: 020 7404 4466
e-mail: office-ldn@london.msf.org
website: www.uk.msf.org